CAMBRIDGE

iELTS Trainer

General Training

Six Practice Tests

2

Cambridge University Press
www.cambridge.org/elt

Cambridge Assessment English
www.cambridgeenglish.org

Information on this title: www.cambridge.org/9781108593663

© Cambridge University Press and UCLES 2019

First published 2019

20 19 18 17 16 15 14 13 12 11 10 9 8 7 6 5 4 3 2 1

Printed in Malaysia by Vivar Printing

A catalogue record for this publication is available from the British Library

ISBN 978-1-108-59366-3 General Training Student's Book with Resources Download
ISBN 978-1-108-56758-9 Academic Student's Book with Resources Download

Cambridge University Press has no responsibility for the persistence or accuracy
of URLs for external or third-party internet websites referred to in this publication,
and does not guarantee that any content on such websites is, or will remain,
accurate or appropriate. Information regarding prices, travel timetables, and other
factual information given in this work is correct at the time of first printing but
Cambridge University Press does not guarantee the accuracy of such information thereafter.

Contents

Introduction

What is IELTS?

The International English Language Testing System (IELTS) is widely recognised as a test of the language ability of candidates who need to study or work where English is the language of communication.

There are two types of IELTS test: the Academic Module (taken for entry to undergraduate or postgraduate studies or for professional reasons) and the General Training Module (taken for entry to vocational or training programmes not at degree level and for immigration purposes). Both modules are made up of four tests – Listening, Reading, Writing and Speaking. The Listening and Speaking tests are the same for both Academic and General Training but the Reading and Writing tests are different.

Who is *IELTS Trainer General Training* for?

This book is suitable for anyone who is preparing to take the IELTS General Training Module. *IELTS Trainer* can be used in class with a teacher, or by students working on their own at home. It is aimed at candidates who would like to achieve a Band Score of 6 or higher. (See section on Scoring on page 6.)

What is *IELTS Trainer General Training*?

This book contains six practice tests for IELTS, each covering the Listening, Reading, Writing and Speaking papers. The practice tests in Guided Tests 1 and 2 are also accompanied by training and advice. All six tests are at the level of the exam.

In Test 1 each part of each paper consists of a training section and an exam practice section:

- The training sections have information and exercises to help you prepare for each part of the paper. In the Listening, Writing and Speaking papers, Test 1 presents and practises grammar, vocabulary and functional language relevant to those papers. This is supported by work on correcting common errors

made by IELTS candidates in the exam, as shown by the **Cambridge Learner Corpus** (see page 6). In Writing, there are extracts from the scripts of IELTS candidates as well as sample answers.

- The exam practice sections consist of the test itself accompanied by step-by-step guidance for each task with tips on strategy and advice linked to the questions. There is a wide range of tasks in the IELTS Listening and Reading papers and the same task may not always appear in the same part of the exam every time. The practice tests reflect this variety and training is given in Tests 1 and 2 in all the major task types which you will come across.

Test 2 contains training for the exam focusing on the task types not covered in Test 1, in addition to a review of the information in Test 1. The training sections are shorter in Test 2 than in Test 1. Test 2 also contains an exam practice section with tips and advice on how to deal with the practice test itself.

Tests 3–6 are complete practice tests without advice or training. They contain variations of the task types in Tests 1 and 2 and cover a wide range of topics and text types. They give you the opportunity to practise the strategies and skills you have acquired while working through Tests 1 and 2.

There is an **Explanatory answer key** (see page 5) for each test available to download from esource.cambridge.org.

How to use *IELTS Trainer General Training*

Test 1 Training

- For each part of the paper (e.g. Listening Part 1, page 10), first read the overview **What is ...?**, describing the type(s) of task which that part may contain. For some parts there is also a section called **What does it test?** which describes, for example, the kind of skills that part of the exam tests (e.g. identifying key facts, understanding speakers' opinions).

- Read through the **Task information**, which describes in detail the particular task type that follows.

- Look at the information marked **Tip**, which gives general advice on exam strategy and language.

- Work through **Useful language** exercises in the Listening, Writing and Speaking sections before tackling the exam tasks on the practice pages. These training exercises help to develop the necessary skills and offer practice directly relevant to the exam tasks in Test 1. Answers to the exercises are in the **Explanatory answer key** (available to download from esource.cambridge.org). Many exercises involve focusing on and correcting common language mistakes made by actual IELTS candidates, as shown by the **Cambridge Learner Corpus** (see page 6).

- Check the boxes marked **Advice**. These give practical help with individual questions.

- In **Listening**, use the audio files available to download with the audioscripts from esource.cambridge.org.

- In Test 1 **Writing**, many exercises are based on language used in IELTS essays in the **Cambridge Learner Corpus** and sample answers written by actual IELTS candidates. There are also sample answers which show what is expected of the best candidates. The **Explanatory answer key** contains answers to the exercises. These training exercises build up to an exam task at the end which is similar to, but not the same as, those in the training exercises.

- In **Speaking**, there are exercises which build into a bank of personalised, useful language for the first part of the test and other exercises which practise the language necessary for the prepared talk and discussion which follow in Parts 2 and 3. These can be used with a partner, or when working alone, for timed practice.

Test 1 Exam practice

- Read the **Action plan** for each task in the Listening, Reading and Writing papers immediately before working through the exam practice task. There are many different task types and the Action plans show how to approach each type in the best way to achieve good marks and avoid wasting time.

- Work through the task, carefully following the steps of the Action plan and making use of the help in the **Tip** information and **Advice** boxes.

- Answers to all items are in the **Explanatory answer key**, which explains why the correct answers are right and others are wrong.

Test 2 Training

- Answer the questions in the **Review** section to remind yourself about each part of the test. If you need to, look back at Test 1 to check your answers.

- Work through the exercises in the Writing and Speaking sections. The Speaking section extends the strategies and skills introduced in Test 1 and adds to the topics which you might be asked about. The Writing section revises the strategies covered in Test 1 and offers further targeted language training exercises. Many of the exercises are based on IELTS candidates' answers from the **Cambridge Learner Corpus**.

Test 2 Exam practice

- Answer the questions in each **Action plan reminder**. These ask you about strategies which were introduced in Test 1. Use the cross-reference to refer back to Test 1 if you need to.

- Read through the **Action plans** for the new task types which weren't in Test 1. Use the **Tip** information and **Advice** boxes to help you do the tasks and the **Explanatory answer key** to check your answers.

Tests 3–6 Exam practice

- Try to do the exam tasks under exam conditions where possible, applying the skills and language learnt in Training Tests 1 and 2.

- For the Speaking paper, it is better to work with a partner so that you can ask each other the questions. If that is not possible, follow the instructions and do all three parts alone. Use a watch and keep to the correct time. Recording the test and listening to it can help you identify language areas which need more practice.

You can do Tests 3–6 in any order, but you should always try to keep to the time recommended for each paper.

The Cambridge Learner Corpus

The Cambridge Learner Corpus (CLC) is a large collection of exam scripts written by students taking Cambridge Assessment English exams around the world. It currently contains over 55 million words and is growing all the time. It forms part of the Cambridge English Corpus and it has been built up by Cambridge University Press and Cambridge Assessment English. The CLC currently contains scripts from over:

- over 220,000 students
- 173 different first languages
- 200 different countries

Exercises and extracts from candidates' answers from Writing in *IELTS Trainer General Training* which are based on the CLC are indicated by this icon: ◉

Other components of *IELTS Trainer General Training*

- The **Explanatory answer key** gives the correct answers, and explains them where necessary (especially in Tests 1 and 2). In some cases, such as multiple-choice questions, it also explains why the other possible answers are wrong.
- The full **Transcripts** for the Listening papers are available to download from esource.cambridge.org.
- **Answer sheets** for the Reading and Listening papers are at the back of the book. Before you take the exam, you should study these so that you know how to mark or write your answers correctly. In Writing, the question paper has plenty of lined space for you to write your answers.
- **Audio** recordings for the Listening papers are available to download from esource.cambridge.org. The listening material is indicated by an icon in *IELTS Trainer General Training*: 🎧

International English Language Testing System (IELTS)

Level of IELTS

You do not pass or fail IELTS. You get a Band Score between 1 and 9. Candidates scoring 9 have fluent, accurate English, with wide-ranging vocabulary. They make very few errors and will be capable of performing in English in professional and academic contexts. Candidates scoring 7 can understand and communicate effectively in English, using some complex language, and although there may be errors, these do not impede communication. A score of 5 or lower means that the candidate has a limited range of language and that errors in grammar, pronunciation, etc. lead to misunderstandings.

Different organisations and institutions publish the Band Score they require for entry.

Scoring

The Listening test contains 40 items and each correct item is given one mark.

The Reading test contains 40 items and each correct item is given one mark. The Academic and General Training Reading Tests are graded to the same level. However, because the texts in the Academic Reading Test are more challenging overall than those in the General Training Test, more questions need to be answered correctly on a General Training Test to receive the same grade.

The Writing test (both Academic and General Training) is marked on the following areas: Task Achievement (for Task 1), Task Response (for Task 2), Coherence and Cohesion, Lexical Resource, Grammatical Range and Accuracy. Examiners give a Band Score for each of these criteria, which are equally weighted.

For the Speaking test, a Band Score is given for each of the following, which are equally weighted: Fluency and Coherence, Lexical Resource, Grammatical Range and Pronunciation.

Candidates receive scores on a Band Scale from 1 to 9 for each skill tested (Listening, Reading, Writing and Speaking). They are of equal importance. These four scores are then averaged and rounded to produce an Overall Band Score. Each candidate receives a Test Report Form setting out their Overall Band Score and their scores for each test. The scores are reported in whole bands or half bands according to the nine-band score given below.

If you do the practice tests in *IELTS Trainer General Training* under exam conditions, you need to score approximately 20 marks on both the Reading and Listening tests for a Band Score of around 5.5. To achieve a Band Score of 7, you need approximately 30 marks in both Reading and Listening.

IELTS Band Scores

9 Expert user – Has fully operational command of the language: appropriate, accurate and fluent with complete understanding.

8 Very good user – Has fully operational command of the language with only occasional unsystematic inaccuracies and inappropriacies. Misunderstandings may occur in unfamiliar situations. Handles complex, detailed argumentation well.

7 Good user – Has operational command of the language, though with occasional inaccuracies, inappropriacies and misunderstandings in some situations. Generally handles complex language well and understands detailed reasoning.

6 Competent user – Has generally effective command of the language despite some inaccuracies, inappropriacies and misunderstandings. Can use and understand fairly complex language, particularly in familiar situations.

5 Modest user – Has partial command of the language, coping with overall meaning in most situations, though is likely to make many mistakes. Should be able to handle basic communication in own field.

4 Limited user – Basic competence is limited to familiar situations. Has frequent problems in understanding and expression. Is not able to use complex language.

3 Extremely limited user – Conveys and understands only general meaning in very familiar situations. Frequent breakdowns in communication occur.

2 Intermittent user – No real communication is possible except for the most basic information using isolated words or short formulae in familiar situations and to meet immediate needs. Has great difficulty understanding spoken and written English.

1 Non-user – Essentially has no ability to use the language beyond possibly a few isolated words.

0 Did not attempt the test – No assessable information provided.

For more information on grading and results, go to the Cambridge Assessment English website (see page 9).

Content of IELTS

IELTS has four papers, each consisting of two, three or four parts. For details on each paper, see below.

Paper 1 Listening about 30 minutes, with 10 minutes at the end to transfer answers to the answer sheet

- This paper is common to both the Academic and General Training Modules.
- The topics in Parts 1 and 2 are based around social situations but the topics in Parts 3 and 4 are all in an educational or training context.
- The **level of difficulty** increases from Part 1 to Part 4.
- Each part is heard **once only**.
- The **instructions** for each task are on the question paper.
- There is a short **pause** before each part which can be used to look at the task and questions. Where there is more than one task in a part, there is also a short pause before the part of the recording which relates to the next task.
- A brief introductory explanation of the **context** is heard before each part, but is **not** printed on the question paper.
- Correct **spelling** is essential on the answer sheet.

Paper 1 Listening about 30 minutes, with 10 minutes at the end to transfer answers to the answer sheet

Part	No. of questions	Text type	Task types *Each part has one or more of these task types*	Task information
1	10	a conversation or interview between two speakers, giving and exchanging information about an everyday topic	table, note and form completion	page 10
2	10	a monologue (sometimes introduced by another speaker) giving information on an everyday topic, e.g. a radio programme or talk from a guide	plan / map labelling	pages 14
			multiple-choice	pages 14, 17
			flow-chart completion	page 17
			sentence completion	page 20
3	10	a conversation between two, three or four speakers in an educational or training context	matching tasks	page 67
4	10	a monologue in an academic setting, e.g. a lecture or presentation		

Paper 2 General Training Reading 1 hour

- This paper is only taken in the General Training Module. There is a different paper for candidates taking the Academic Module (see Cambridge Assessment English website). Both papers follow the same format but the kinds of texts on the two modules differ in terms of topic, genre, complexity of language and style.

- There are approximately 2,750 words in total in the three passages.

Passage	No. of questions	Text types	Task types *Each passage has one or more of these task types*	Task information and practice
1	13 (two or three tasks)	Texts may be from 'social survival 'sources such as notices,advertisements timetables, or 'workplace survival' sources such as job descriptions work development and training or 'general reading' such as newspapers, magazines and fictional and non-fictional book extracts.	true / false / not given	page 23
			locating information	page 23
2	13 (three tasks)		note completion	page 29
			sentence completion	page 29
3	14 (three tasks)		multiple-choice	page 36
			matching headings	page 36
			summary completion	page 36
			flow-chart completion	page 84
			matching places	page 88

Paper 3 General Training Writing 1 hour

This paper is only taken in the General Training Module. There is a different paper for candidates taking the Academic Module (see Cambridge Assessment English website).

Task	Suggested time and marks	Task text type and no. of words	Task information
1	20 minutes one-third of the marks for the paper	a presentation of a situation which requires the writing of a letter or email requesting information or giving an explanation. The letter may be personal, semi-formal or formal in style. 150 words minimum	pages 43–50
2	40 minutes two-thirds of the marks for the paper	an essay in response to a point of view, argument or problem. The essay can be fairly personal in style. 250 words minimum	pages 51–57

Paper 4 Speaking 11–14 minutes

This paper is common to both the Academic and General Training Modules.

It is a face-to-face interview with an examiner and it is recorded.

Part	Time	Task type	Task information
1	4–5 minutes	giving personal information and discussing everyday subjects	pages 58–59
2	1 minute preparation 2 minutes talk	giving a prepared talk on a subject given by the examiner and answering one or two follow-up questions	pages 60–61
3	4–5 minutes	a discussion with the examiner arising from the topic of Part 2, offering the opportunity to discuss more abstract issues and ideas	page 62

Further information

The information about IELTS contained in *IELTS Trainer General Training* is designed to be an overview of the exam. For a full description of IELTS, including information about task types, testing focus and preparation for the exam, please see the *IELTS Handbook*, which can be obtained from Cambridge Assessment English at the address below or from the website at: www.cambridgeenglish.org.

Cambridge Assessment English

The Triangle Building

Shaftesbury Road

Cambridge CB2 8EA

United Kingdom

What is Listening Part 1?

- a conversation between two people, either face to face or on the phone
- one or two tasks (e.g. table completion)
- an example and 10 questions

The purpose of the conversation is to communicate and share information that will be useful in some way (e.g. for making a holiday booking, for working out the best transport options).

What does it test?

- understanding specific information e.g. dates, prices, everyday objects, locations
- spelling of people and place names

Task information: *Table, Note and Form completion*

This task requires you to fill in the spaces in the table. The spaces are numbered in the same order as the information you hear.

You have to:

- listen to a conversation, which you hear once only.
- write one to three words, a number, or a date in each space in the table.
- write the exact words you hear.
- spell everything correctly.

Useful language: spelling

In Part 1, a speaker will sometimes spell out the name of a person, street or company.

You need to be very familiar with the English names for the letters of the alphabet, as the word will only be spelt out once.

01 **1** **Listen and choose the first letter in each pair that you hear.**

1	A / E	**2**	A / I	**3**	E / I	**4**	A / R
5	Y / E	**6**	O / U	**7**	B / P	**8**	G / J
9	S / F	**10**	M / N	**11**	H / X	**12**	D / T

> **Advice**
>
> *Not all place names are spelt out. For example, the underlined words are very common in English, so you should learn how to spell words like these.*
>
> *<u>Mountain</u> View Hotel*
> *<u>Ocean</u> Road*
> *<u>Bridge</u> Street*

02 **2** **Listen to some words being spelt out and write down what you hear.**

1 Manager: Sarah ....
2 Email: .... @gmail.com
3 Meeting point: .... School sports field
4 Hotel name: ....
5 Address: 112 .... Terrace
6 Company: .... Movers

Useful language: numbers

03 **1** **Listen and write the numbers you hear.**

1 Customer cell phone: ....
2 Distance of race: .... miles
3 A one-way ticket is: ....
4 Home address: .... Bayside Road.
5 Width of window frame: .... inches
6 Booking reference: ....

> **Advice**
>
> *When we say a phone number, we can pronounce 0 as **oh**, or say **zero**.*
>
> *When we talk about money we say, for example, **seven pounds / dollars / euros fifty**. (£7.50, $7.50, €7.50).*

 TIP The answer can be written in numerals or in letters, e.g. 650, or six hundred and fifty. But it's much easier and faster to write numerals!

TIP For similar sounding numbers, listen out for the stressed syllable e.g. fif<u>teen</u>, <u>fif</u>ty, six<u>teen</u>, <u>six</u>ty.

Useful language: times and dates

1 Listen and write the times or dates you hear.

04

1 Arrival date: ....

2 Class schedule: .... to 6:30 p.m.

3 Date of last inspection: ...., 2018

4 Best time to visit: ....

5 The courses finishes on: ....

6 Delivery date: ....

Advice

We say dates like 1752 or 1997 as **seventeen fifty-two** *and* **nineteen ninety-seven**. *For years following 2000, we can say, for example,* **two thousand eighteen**, *or* **two thousand and /ən/ eighteen**, *or* **twenty eighteen**.

Useful language: recognising when the answer is coming

In Part 1, you might see a question like 'Height: about **1**................cm'. You might not hear the word 'height' in the recording. Instead, the speaker might ask a question, or say something that relates to a person's height. This will tell you when the answer is coming.

TIP You can write a date in different ways to get a mark (e.g. 3rd March, March 3 or 3 March). This fits the **one word and / or a number** in the instruction.

1 Match an answer 1–6 with a question A–F the speaker might ask.

Height: around **1** ......*6*...... feet	**A** 'So can you tell me how long the curtains are?'
Width: **2** ...*15*... centimetres	**B** 'How tall are the trees at the moment – approximately?'
Distance: **3** ...*26*... kilometres	**C** 'And what would the charge for that be?'
Length: **4** ...*330*... inches	**D** 'How heavy is the box you want us to move?'
Weight: about **5** ...*63*... kg	**E** 'Do you know how wide the screen is?'
Cost: **6** $ ...*560*...	**F** 'How far is it from the hotel to the airport?'

TIP Don't add words like **euros** or **inches** or **kilometres** to the answer sheet if they are provided on the question paper.

Useful strategy: deciding what to write in the spaces

1 Look at the sample exam task below and complete this table.

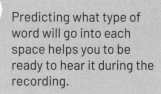

TIP Predicting what type of word will go into each space helps you to be ready to hear it during the recording.

Which space needs ...		What tells you this?
a date?	8	*the verb 'starts' and 'Wednesday'.*
a price?		
a phone number?		
a person's name		
a period of time?		
a place?		
a piece of equipment or clothing – singular noun?		
a piece of equipment or clothing – plural noun?		
a verb / action?		
a part of the body?		

Advice

*Speakers sometimes mention a time, date or number, which might fit a space, but is not the real answer. This is called a **distraction**. Listen carefully in case the speaker changes their mind, or another speaker corrects them with the real time, date or number.*

Westwood Community Centre Activities

Classes: when / where
Yoga basics
Example:
Mondays 7 p.m. – *8:30* p.m.
Taking place in the hall

Things to bring
a **1** .... is necessary for every session

Other information
Discounted rate for students:
2 $ ....

Simple techniques that will help you
3 .... pain in your **4** ....

Classes: when / where
Westwood Walkers
7:00 a.m. every morning

The walk starts from outside the
5 .... in the village

Things to bring
A good pair of
6 .... will help

Other information
Free for everyone

The organiser is **7** ....
Lindsay

Classes: when / where
Cycle Group
Training starts again on
Wednesday, **8** ....

The rides take about
9 .... on average

Things to bring
helmet and bike lights are essential

Other information
No charge

Nicky's contact details:
10 ....

Action plan for *Table completion*

1 Look at the instructions to find out how many words you can write.
2 Look at the heading and the subheadings. There is time to do this before you listen.
3 Look at the spaces and think about what kinds of word or number are needed (e.g. a date, a distance, an address, a plural noun).
4 Listen to the introduction, which tells you what the conversation is about.
5 Listen carefully to the conversation and focus on each question in turn. As soon as you've written the answer to one question, listen for the answer to the next.
6 Move on to the next row each time the speaker talks about something new – in this case, a new class.

TIP Write an answer in each space even if you aren't sure about it. A guess might turn out to be right and get a mark, but an empty space won't be given a mark.

TIP The question numbers run horizontally across each row.

TIP If one of your answers is more than one word and a number, it is wrong, and won't get a mark.

🎧 05 Questions 1–10

Complete the table below.

*Write **ONE WORD AND / OR A NUMBER** for each answer.*

TIP Remember you only hear the recording once.

Art classes at Bramley Community Centre

Class	Things to bring	Fees / Timetable	Tutor
Example 'Movement and (light)': painting in the style of French Impressionists	a set of 1 ...supplies... *(describe)* is essential (brushes) ✓	The cost is 170 2 $ ..285... for two terms Monday evenings 6–8 p.m., Room 15	A local artist called Steve 3 .... RAMDHANIE ✓
'Clay basics': using the pottery wheel to make several 4 ..Simph.. balls bowls	an old 5 ..shirt.. clothe would be a good idea	The cost is $180 per term Every 6 ..Wednesday.. thursday 6:30–8:30 p.m., Room 3	Theresa Clark – her work is displayed in the community centre
'Sketching Architecture': drawing old buildings, starting with the 7 ..Paris.. Paris library	people usually take a fold-up chair and a 8 ..sandwich.. ✓	The cost is $160 per term Fridays 11–1 p.m. meet at the corner of Victoria Street and 9 .... Road station ✓	Annie Li Annie's cell phone number: 10 .... 021 785 6361 ✓

Advice

1 *Should the noun you write be plural or singular?*
2 *Make sure the answer you choose is for two terms, not one.*
4 *Use your general knowledge to predict the kind of things people might make in a pottery class. And note the word **several**.*
5 *Listen for the word **old**, a similar adjective, or a paraphrase in the recording. This may signal that the answer is coming soon. Note that the occurrence of the same adjective (old) in both the recording and the question is unusual.*
6 *What does the word **every** tell you about the kind of noun that is needed?*
7 *The answer must be a kind of building. Listen carefully – because one or more buildings might be mentioned as distraction.*

What is Listening Part 2?

- a talk / speech / announcement / recorded message / radio excerpt given by one person, sometimes with an introduction by another person
- usually two tasks (e.g. multiple-choice, matching, flow-chart completion, plan / map labelling)
- 10 questions; there is a brief pause in the recording before the start of the next task

Task information: *Plan / map labelling*

Plan / map labelling requires you to transfer the information you hear to a simple plan / map. You need to follow language expressing where things are located.

You have to:

- listen to part of the talk, which you hear once only.
- match a list of places to their locations (labelled A, B, C etc.) on the plan / map.
- write A, B, C etc. next to the corresponding place in the list.

The speaker's purpose is to provide information that will be useful in some way (e.g. to inform staff about new health and safety requirements, to give directions to a group of volunteers, to tell people about a local event they could attend).

What does it test?

- identifying specific factual information and detail
- understanding stated opinion

Task information: *5-option multiple-choice*

Multiple-choice questions usually focus on the details. The questions follow the order of the recording, although the options A–E do not.

You have to:

- listen to the recording, which you'll hear only once.
- choose two options from a list of five, i.e. A–E.

There is another kind of multiple-choice task – see Test 1 Part 3.

Useful language: *plan / map labelling* tasks

For Part 2, you will need to recognise language for directions.

1   Look at the places marked on the plan. Complete the sentences with phrases from the box. (Usually there are not so many labelled buildings on the map, or complete sentences.)

at the top	directly below	in between	in the centre	just above	nearest to
right-hand corner	smaller of	square-shaped	surrounded by	the south	to the right

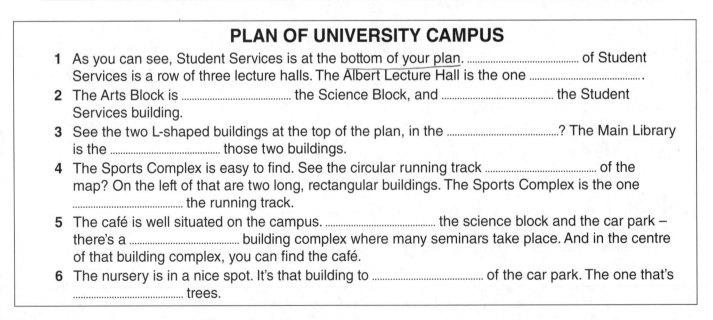

PLAN OF UNIVERSITY CAMPUS

1   As you can see, Student Services is at the bottom of your plan. .... of Student Services is a row of three lecture halls. The Albert Lecture Hall is the one ....

2   The Arts Block is .... the Science Block, and .... the Student Services building.

3   See the two L-shaped buildings at the top of the plan, in the ....? The Main Library is the .... those two buildings.

4   The Sports Complex is easy to find. See the circular running track .... of the map? On the left of that are two long, rectangular buildings. The Sports Complex is the one .... the running track.

5   The café is well situated on the campus. .... the science block and the car park – there's a .... building complex where many seminars take place. And in the centre of that building complex, you can find the café.

6   The nursery is in a nice spot. It's that building to .... of the car park. The one that's .... trees.

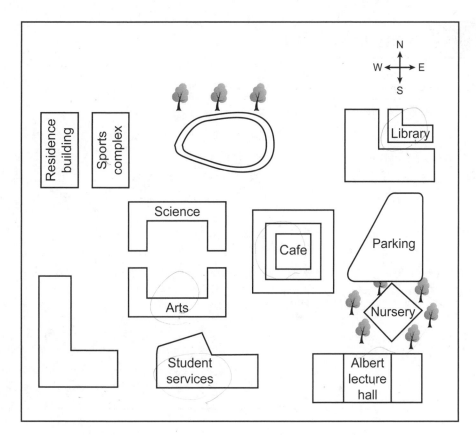

2 Listen and check your answers.

06

Useful strategy: paraphrasing in *5-option multiple-choice* tasks

In many IELTS tasks, you have to choose a correct answer from a number of options. The options may use different language to express ideas mentioned in the recording. This is known as 'paraphrasing'.

1 Match options A–E with extracts 1–5.

Underline the parts of the extracts that match the underlined phrases in the options.

A <u>dealing with</u> <u>unhappy clients</u> on the phone

B improving <u>written</u> <u>communication skills</u>

C giving <u>presentations</u> to <u>colleagues</u>

D filing <u>documents</u> <u>correctly</u>

E <u>being a mentor</u> <u>to junior members of staff</u>

1 So one thing the session will cover is how to deal with the huge amount of paperwork we receive. In other words, how we organise and store it all, in the right way, I mean.

2 I've been impressed by the way you've all managed to stand up and deliver a talk to the other people on your team. I don't think we need any more training in that area for now.

3 When a dissatisfied customer rings you up to complain, you need to know how to handle the situation effectively. We dealt with this in the previous session.

4 As you know, we have a number of trainees starting work next week. We don't have time to talk about this in the training session, but I'd like you to support and guide them during their first few months in the company.

5 From time to time you need to produce formal reports and the aim of this training session is to show you how to express your ideas more effectively and clearly.

Action plan for *5-option multiple-choice*

1 Read the questions so you know what kind of information you need to listen for.

2 Underline key words and ideas in the options and remember these may be paraphrased in the recording.

3 Listen to the introduction. It tells you who is speaking and describes the situation.

4 Transfer your answers to the answer sheet at the end of the test.

> **TIP** You can write the two options in any order on the answer sheet (e.g. A / B or B / A)

Questions 11–12

07 *Choose **TWO** letters, **A–E**.*

*Which **TWO** things will employees need to do during their first week in their new office space?*

A find out about safety procedures

B collect a new form of identification

C move boxes containing documents

D make a note of any problem that occurs

E learn about new company technology

> **Advice**
>
> **11–12** Listen out for ideas which might be paraphrased in the options. Make sure the options you choose match exactly what the speaker says.
>
> **13–14** The options may not be in the same order as in the recording. Cross them off when you think they have been paraphrased.

Questions 13–14

*Choose **TWO** letters, **A–E**.*

*Which **TWO** steps have the company taken to improve the physical environment of employees' offices?*

A provided comfortable seating

B installed a new heating system

C used attractive materials

D enlarged people's working space

E replaced the old type of lights

Action plan for *Plan / map labelling*

1 Read the instructions and the list of places you have to locate.

2 Quickly scan the plan for places, buildings or objects already labelled.

3 Identify any useful features that might be mentioned in the talk, e.g. a bridge, and look for arrows for north, south, etc.

4 As you listen, write the letters (**A, B, C**, etc.) next to the list of places.

5 Transfer your answers to the answer sheet at the end of the Listening test.

> **TIP** The speaker will use the same place names you see in the list. These won't be paraphrased in any way.

> **TIP** The letters on the plan are not in the same order as the places you hear mentioned, but the places in the numbered questions are.

Questions 15–20

07 *Label the plan below.*

*Write the correct letter, **A–I**, next to **Questions 15–20**.*

Plan of the renovated factory complex

15 Conference centre   ....

16 New office space   ....

17 Stores   ....

18 Finance   ....

19 Café   ....

20 IT department   ....

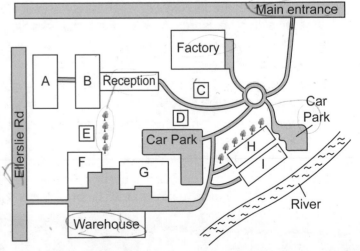

What is Listening Part 3?

- a discussion between two or sometimes three speakers (e.g. between one or more students and / or their university tutor)
- two tasks (e.g. flow-chart, multiple-choice or matching)
- 10 questions, with a brief pause in the discussion between the parts that relate to each task

The subject is an aspect of academic life (e.g. a presentation).

Task information: *3-option multiple-choice*

In Part 3, this task usually focuses on attitude / opinion, negotiation and (dis)agreement.

You have to:
- listen to the recording, which you will hear once only.
- choose from options **A**, **B** or **C** to answer a question or complete a statement so that it means the same as the information in the recording.

Useful strategy: identifying the locating words

In many IELTS tasks you need to identify the words (e.g. in the notes, flow-chart or questions) which are also in the recording. These words will help you follow a conversation and know which part of it contains the information you need.

Locating words are usually dates or statistics, names objects or events, which are difficult to paraphrase.

1   Underline the locating words in questions 1–6.

History of antibiotics

Fleming's discovery of penicillin in 1928 reduced people's fear of **1** ....

↓

pharmaceutical companies realised antibiotics like penicillin and chloramphenicol could lead to **2** ....

↓

jungles and mountain areas were explored for **3** ....

↓

manufacturers in the US and Europe decided to focus on **4** .... instead

↓

5 .... have offered a limited range of antibiotics since the 1970s

↓

some **6** .... no longer respond to antibiotics, with 700,000 cases annually

What does it test?

- identifying key facts and ideas and how they relate to each other
- identifying speakers' attitudes and opinions
- recognising agreement and disagreement

Task information: *Flow-chart completion*

Flow-chart completion requires you to follow the development of a discussion. The steps in the flow-chart are in the same order as what you hear.

You have to:
- listen to part of the discussion, which you hear once only.
- choose one option (**A**, **B**, **C**, etc.) from the box to complete each space in the flow-chart according to what you hear.

Vocabulary

For Part 3 flow-charts, the vocabulary in the options will be different to the language you hear in the recording.

1   Look at these examples of language from the recording on the history of antibiotics. Match them with options A–I.

1   the financial gain would be enormous. ☐
2   clinics and hospitals ☐
3   people receiving medical care ☐
4   specimens of microorganisms ☐
5   artificial kinds of antibiotic ☐
6   a cut that went septic / a sore throat ☐
7   a real improvement ☐
8   doctors and surgeons ☐
9   severe illness ☐

A	synthetic forms	F	bacteria samples
B	serious diseases	G	treatment centres
C	genuine progress	H	sick patients
D	common infections	I	large profits
E	medical professionals		

🎧 08   **2   Listen to some extracts. Complete the flow-chart with options A–I.**

Useful strategy: *3-option multiple-choice*

For Part 3, these questions may test understanding of agreement and disagreement.

1 Look at the list of phrases.

Decide whether they suggest agreement ☑, or disagreement ☒.

1 Actually, you could be right. ☐

2 I doubt it. ☐

3 I hardly think so. ☐

4 Fair enough. ☐

5 I couldn't agree more. ☐

6 Precisely. ☐

7 I'm not sure I go along with that. ☐

8 That's one way of looking at it, but … ☐

9 You have a point there. ☐

10 Exactly. ☐

11 Come on. Surely that's not the case. ☐

12 Not necessarily. ☐

Exam Practice Test 1 | Listening Part 3

Action plan for *Flow-chart completion*

1 Read the instructions and check how many spaces there are in the flow-chart.

2 Look at the heading of the flow-chart to find out the discussion topic.

3 Look at the flow-chart and underline the locating words.

4 Read the list of options, and remember they will probably be paraphrased in the recording.

5 Listen carefully to the conversation, and be ready for the answer when you hear the locating words.

6 Transfer your answers to the answer sheet at the end of the test.

TIP The question numbers run horizontally across each row.

TIP Many of the options fit in several spaces. Don't try and guess the answers.

TIP Focus on each question in turn. As soon as you have answered one question, look at the next stage of the flow-chart.

🎧 **Questions 21–26**

09 *Complete the flow-chart below.*

*Choose **SIX** answers from the box and write the correct letter, **A–I**, next to **Questions 21–26**.*

A lifestyle changes

B famous people

C scientific findings

D industrial processes

E poor diet

F effective packaging

G toxic substances

H processed foods

I alarming images

Advice

A–I *These options may be mentioned in any order. Three of them will not be needed.*

21 *Listen for the date as the answer will come shortly afterwards.*

23 Governments *is the locating word.* **Popularity** *is expressed using different language in the recording.*

24 *Both **1940s** and **housewives** are useful locating words.*

25 *How might **more accessible to consumers** be paraphrased?*

26 *What's another way of saying **rise**? The answer will come after one of the speakers has said this.*

History of vitamin supplements

Prior to 1900s: physical weakness is thought to be caused by **21** ....

↓

Early 1900s: research shows a link between **22** .... and sickness

↓

1930s: governments become concerned about the popularity of **23** ....

↓

1940s: **24** .... convince housewives to buy vitamin supplements

↓

1950s: **25** .... make vitamin supplements more accessible to consumers

↓

1960s to present day: vitamin supplement sales continue to rise because of **26** ....

Action Plan for *3-option multiple-choice*

1 Read the questions. They give you an idea of what information you should listen for.

2 Underline the locating words in the questions.

3 Quickly read through the A, B, C options, remembering that these will be paraphrased in the recording.

4 As soon as you've chosen the answer to a question, listen for the answer to the next one.

5 Check your answers and transfer them to the answer sheet at the end of the Listening test.

TIP Underline locating words that are unique to each question.

Questions 27–30

09

Choose the correct letter, A, B or C.

27 Sam believes that more Australians are taking vitamin supplements because they

   A want to have control of their own health.

   B are advised to by local health authorities.

   C have benefitted from competition amongst manufacturers.

28 Lucy is concerned that the US vitamin supplement industry is not required to

   A follow the guidelines produced by a government agency.

   B list all the possible side effects of taking vitamins.

   C provide evidence that their products are effective.

29 When discussing the Danish experiment, Lucy and Sam conclude that vitamin supplements

   A are best used for preventing minor illnesses.

   B are not fully understood by researchers.

   C are harmful if taken in large amounts.

30 Lucy and Sam agree that stricter regulation of the vitamin supplement industry

   A would only lead to a slight decrease in sales.

   B might be necessary for some types of vitamin.

   C may not be welcomed by all consumers.

Advice

27 Choose the option that reflects Sam's personal opinion, not just an idea he refers to.

28 The options do not follow the order of the information Lucy gives.

29 **Minor illnesses**, **scientists** and **harmful** are all paraphrased in the recording. But the option you choose must exactly reflect Lucy and Sam's conclusion.

30 Listen for phrases of agreement and disagreement to help you choose the right option.

What is Listening Part 4?

- a lecture, talk or presentation given by one speaker, usually in front of an audience
- one or two tasks e.g. note completion, sentence completion
- 10 questions

The subject is a topic of academic interest (e.g. a scientific or historical subject).

What does it test?

- understanding and distinguishing between ideas: reasons, causes, effects, consequences, etc.
- following the way the ideas are organised (e.g. main ideas, specific information, attitude) and the speaker's opinion
- accurate spelling

Task information: *Sentence completion*

This task requires you to fill in the spaces in a set of sentences. It is almost identical to note completion. The sentences are in the same order as the information you hear.

For this task you have to:

- listen to a talk, once only.
- read the instructions so you know how many words you may write.
- write the exact words you hear.
- spell everything correctly.

Vocabulary: environmental issues and collocation

1   Underline the correct word in each sentence.
    1   *Habitat / Area / Land loss* is the biggest threat to wildlife in the region.
    2   The white rhino is high on the list of critically *risky / endangered / rare* species.
    3   Leftover food accounts for a high proportion of *household / dwelling / residence* waste.
    4   Governments are now investing in *recycled / renewable / reused* energy such as solar power.
    5   Don't take so many flights if you want to reduce your carbon *footprint / steps / tracks*.
    6   Vehicle *releases / productions / emissions* are largely responsible for the rise in asthma rates.
    7   Most scientists say global *heating / warming / melting* is a consequence of human activity.
    8   At some point, we will certainly run out of fossil *energies / powers / fuels*.

Useful strategy: signposting

For Part 4 lectures and talks, a speaker may sometimes use signposting language to show they are moving on to a new aspect of the topic e.g.
- 'Now let's turn to…'
- 'Moving on, let's now think about…'

The speaker may also ask a question or make a statement that
- paraphrases a subheading in the Notes.
- uses many of the same words from the subheading.

1   Read the subheadings 1–5 in the *Note completion* task below. Match the subheadings with the examples of signposting A–E. You do not need to fill the gaps.

The future of the world's trees

1   **Trees and their commercial use**
   • We need trees for
      – construction materials   – the .... industry

2   **Trees in the ecosystem**
   • Trees provide a range of species with both
      – a food source   – opportunities for ....

3   **The ways that trees can affect our general happiness**
   • Researchers have proved that living near to trees
      – reduces the amount of .... that people have
      – encourages better relations between ....

4   **The reasons why different tree species are dying out**
   • Diseases are often spread because
      – the restrictions on .... are not enough
      – some people ignore the rules about entering ....

5   **Solutions for saving the trees**
   • Scientists need to share their data on ....
   • Greater funding must be given to the collection of ....

Signposting examples
   A   Well, there are a number of reasons why various species of tree are dying out.
   B   So what can we do about this problem? There are a number of ways that ….
   C   Let's think about the role trees play in the wider environment. Many birds and animals ….
   D   Let's start with an overview of how trees are used by manufacturers.
   E   Another way that trees are useful to us relates to the impact they have on our overall wellbeing, that is to say, how they influence our emotional health.

Useful language: cause and effect

In Part 4, the questions may test your understanding of cause and effect.

1   Decide if the <u>underlined phrase</u> is followed by cause or effect.
   1   Plastic pollution <u>has led to</u> a number of marine species being threatened.
   2   <u>Due to</u> a rise in air temperature, the polar caps are melting faster than ever before.
   3   The same fields have been used to produce crops for decades. <u>The result of this</u> has been poor soil quality.
   4   <u>Since</u> we haven't received enough funding for the project, we'll need to raise money ourselves.
   5   Organic food sales are going up <u>owing to the fact</u> that people don't want food sprayed with insecticide.
   6   Gorillas have lost much of their natural habitat, <u>meaning</u> that they are struggling to survive.

Action plan for *Sentence completion*

1 Look at the instructions and check how many words you must write in each space.

2 Read the questions (the sentences) carefully, identifying the locating words.

3 Listen and complete each space with the exact words you hear.

4 Before you transfer your answers to the answer sheet, check that the completed sentence makes sense.

 TIP The locating words may appear anywhere in a question, but you will hear them before the answer in the recording.

 TIP Listen out for examples of signposting that tell you when to move on to a new set of questions.

 Questions 31–36

10 *Complete the notes below.*

*Write **NO MORE THAN TWO WORDS** for each answer.*

Insect Extinction in the 21st Century

The reasons why insect populations are declining

- In Europe, important plants are no longer found in fields or **31** ....
- In the Amazon rainforest, **32** .... might be the cause of butterfly and beetle loss.
- Globally, pesticides are affecting the spatial skills and **33** .... of bees.

The consequences of declining insect populations

- Insects are an essential part of the **34** .... in all places apart from Antarctica.
- Crop production will fall dramatically.
- Researchers can't discover any new **35** ....based on plants.

The possible ways to prevent insect extinction

- Governments must restrict the sale of pesticides.
- People must reduce their consumption of **36** ....

Questions 37–40

Complete the sentences below.

*Write **ONE WORD ONLY** for each answer.*

37 Sand from the Antioch Dunes was used to make .... for houses in the early 1900s.

38 The metalmark butterfly requires one type of Antioch Dunes plant for its ....

39 In recent years .... has led to the loss of wildlife in the Antioch Dunes.

40 The Antioch Dunes project shows how .... does not always require much land.

Advice

37 *What kind of things do builders sometimes need to make for houses?*

38 *Why do butterflies need plants? Think of some different reasons.*

39 *You need to listen out for a cause i.e. the reason why wildlife has decreased.*

40 *The auxiliary **does**, and the lack of an article (a / an), shows you that the answer must be an uncountable noun.*

What is Reading Passage 1?

- two to three texts, one of which may consist of 6–8 short texts related by topic, e.g. hotel advertisements
- two or three tasks, with a total of 14 questions
- usually slightly easier than Passages 2 and 3

What does it test?

- understanding texts that are relevant to everyday life in an English-speaking country
- the ability to retrieve and provide general factual information, e.g. notices or advertisements

Task information: *True / False / Not given*

True / False / Not given tasks require you to compare the information given in a series of statements with information given in the text and decide if they are the same.

You have to:
- read statements which are in the same order as the information in the text.
- scan the text to find the information you need.
- decide if the idea given in each statement agrees with the text (*True*), or contradicts the text (*False*), or if there is no information about it in the text (*Not given*).

Task information: *Locating information*

Locating information requires you to scan a text (often made up of several short parts, e.g. advertisements) to find specific information in one part.

You have to:
- read a text that is divided into parts or paragraphs or 6–8 very short independent texts.
- read statements that focus on details in one part or paragraph.
- find which part or paragraph contains the information in each question. The answer may be in one sentence or phrase or you may need to read more than one sentence.

1 **Read the text below (skim the text). What is it? Choose a, b or c.**

a Instructions for camping at night

b Information about activities offered at a zoo

c Details of animals' habitats

Sleeping over at the zoo

This overnight camping adventure is perfect for school and youth groups. Sleepover activities are aligned with National Science Standards. Each program includes:

- Live animal presentations
- Zoo craft activity
- Breakfast and beverages
- A guide who will show you the nocturnal animals and stay at the camp

Adult/Child Ratio

- Minimum adult to child ratio of 1:4.
- Maximum adult to child ratio of 1:1.

Set up your zoo tent at 'Camp Kenya'.
Pricing starts at $90 per camper (students and adults).
Hot catered meals are available for an additional fee.

2 **Look at the instructions for Questions 1–7 below and circle the key words.**

Questions 1–7

Do the following statements agree with the information given in Passage 1?

In boxes 1–7 on your answer sheet, write

TRUE	*if the statement agrees with the information*
FALSE	*if the statement contradicts the information*
NOT GIVEN	*if there is no information on this*

1 The activities are designed to be educational.

2 Guides will help with putting up tents.

3 The $90 sleepover fee includes an evening meal.

4 There must be an adult present for every four children that attend.

5 Breakfast includes a vegetarian option.

6 Activities offered are arts and science based.

7 Adults and children pay the same fee.

3 **Look at the text and underline where the information is given for each statement. Some information is not given for some of the statements.**

Now, answer **Questions 1–7** in Exercise 2.

*You should spend about 20 minutes on **Questions 1–14**, which are based on the two reading passages below.*

*Read the text below and answer **Questions 1–7**.*

Marxland Sculpture Garden:
Information for Visitors

A brief history

The Marxland Sculpture Garden occupies 30 hectares of land to the north of the historical town of Coppard. A former golf course, the land was bought by the Coppard Council in 1971 and, thanks to a generous donation by the Marxland
family, opened to the public as a sculpture garden in 1975.

What to see

The Garden features more than 120 outdoor sculptures, though areas of the grounds themselves are also works of art, thanks to the efforts of landscape designer Hugh O'Connor. There are both permanent and temporary exhibits, many of which were created by artists from the region, most notably renowned bronze sculptor, Nerida Graham. As you wander through the grounds, don't miss *Shackle of Time*, the colossal mechanical sculpture in the Succulent Garden, or *Figurine* near the pond.

Your visit

The main car park is at the North Street entrance – open 9:00 to 17:00.

If approaching from the east, we also have a smaller parking area available at the Gray Street entrance.

The Marxland Sculpture Garden is open seven days a week 10:00–16:30, excluding 25 and 26 December.

Winter months: The Garden closes at 20:30 for 'Marxland at Night'.

Entry: $15 per adult, $10 per child (under 14); $40 for a family day pass.

The Marxland Sculpture Garden is a hands-on experience so don't be afraid to get up close and feel the surface of the works. We just ask that visitors don't climb on any of the exhibits.

Extra events

There's always something happening at the Garden.

The Jazz in the Garden festival is held in the second week of April, boasting world-class musicians and fantastic food stalls. This is the first time it has been held over two days. The festival has increased in popularity every year since it began in the early 1980s, so get your tickets early!

The Garden has recently started its 'Marxland at Night' program, featuring magical illuminated sculptures. Take an organised tour with one of the Garden staff or try your luck with a map and torch! This event takes place throughout winter.

Action plan for *True / False / Not given*

1 Look at the title and any headings and decide what the text is about.

2 Read the text very quickly to get an idea of what it is about. Don't worry about words you don't understand.

3 Look at the questions and underline the important words.

4 Find the part of the text which mentions the information in the first question. Read that part carefully and decide if the answer is *True, False* or *Not given*.

5 Now do the same for the other questions.

TIP The information you need comes in the same order as the information in the text, but it is not always evenly spaced through the text. Some information in the text corresponding to questions may be closer together and some further apart.

TIP The information in the questions will be a paraphrase of what is in the text, so do not expect to find all the same words. Look for synonyms and phrases that have a similar meaning.

TIP There will always be at least one *True*, one *False* and one *Not given* answer. However, there may not be the same number of each answer.

Advice

1 *The heading 'A brief history' indicates there may be information about the use of the garden in the past. Which words refer to a sport and past use?*

3 *Find the name Nerida Graham in the text. Does it specifically say she created 'Shackle of Time'?*

7 *Which words in the final paragraph refer to 'after dark'? Using a synonym will help you find the relevant information. Is a guided tour the only option?*

Questions 1–7

Do the following statements agree with the information given in Reading Passage 1?

In boxes 1–7 on your answer sheet, write

TRUE	*if the statement agrees with the information*
FALSE	*if the statement contradicts the information*
NOT GIVEN	*if there is no information on this*

1 People once played sport on the land used for Marxland Sculpture Garden.

2 Some sculptures are in the park for a limited time.

3 Nerida Graham created the *Shackle of Time* sculpture.

4 It is free to park your car at the gardens.

5 Visitors are forbidden to touch some of the sculptures.

6 Jazz in the Garden has been running for several years.

7 If visiting the park after dark, you must go with a Garden employee.

*Read the text below and answer **Questions 8–14**.*

Cookbooks

A

My Petite Kitchen Cookbook

Eleanor Ozich

Petite Kitchen blogger Eleanor Ozich has produced this collection of over 100 simple, wholesome recipes to nourish you and your family. With a focus on wholefoods, Ozich uses unprocessed alternatives to the usual sugar, milk and processed grains to create more nutritionally-balanced meals. This book contains achievable recipes for home cooks.

B

Ottolenghi: The Cookbook

Sami Tamimi, Yotam Ottolenghi

The iconic restaurant Ottolenghi is known for its exquisite, fresh food that has impacted diners' palettes across the country. Much of the intriguing yet simple fare in the book is taken from recipes that featured in chef Yotam Ottolenghi's childhood in Jerusalem, but other recipes come from different culinary traditions, from North African to Californian. If you enjoy top-notch photos of exotic delicacies, this is for you.

C

Crunch Time Cookbook

Michelle Bridges

In the *Crunch Time Cookbook*, celebrity trainer Bridges arms readers with simple, delicious recipes to help shed kilos and keep them off. There's a 12-week menu plan (also available as an e-book) that shows how quick and cheap it can be to prepare your own meals, and all the recipes are family–friendly.

D

The Smitten Kitchen Cookbook

Deb Perelman

This award-winning cookbook is brought to you by celebrated food blogger Deb Perelman. While not an experienced chef or restaurant owner, Perelman is a home cook who was overwhelmed by the sheer volume of recipes on the internet, sometimes giving conflicting advice. If this sounds like you, this book will give you confidence. Each recipe comes with a photograph, so you can see what you're aiming for.

E

The Classic Slow Cooker

Judy Hannemann

This beautifully-presented collection of tried-and-tested recipes was gathered by Hannemann over the years. Apparently, kids love these simple but tasty ideas. From fresh nutritious appetizers to delicious desserts, here are recipes you'll want to cook again and again.

F

The Wagamama Cookbook

Hugo Arnold

The distinctive taste of the Wagamama restaurant chain originates from the traditional ramen (noodle) shops of Japan. This cookbook contains the key to achieving the Wagamama flavour, from appetisers to hearty soups to stir-fries, and even exotic juice-based beverages. There are also helpful hints on sourcing ingredients, techniques for food preparation and creating a meal.

Action plan for *Locating information*

1 Look at the title and any headings and decide what the mini-texts are about.

2 Read the questions very quickly and see what you can predict about the mini-texts.

3 Read the mini-texts very quickly to get a general idea of what they are about.

4 Read each question carefully, underline the important information and find the mini-text which contains the same information as the question.

5 Check that the information in the question and the mini-text is exactly the same. There is only one correct answer for each question.

TIP Some mini-texts may not contain any answers, while others may contain more than one answer.

TIP The information in the questions will be a paraphrase of what is in the mini-text, so look for words that have a similar meaning.

Advice

11 *A, C and E all mention nutrition or weight loss, but which one discusses using healthy options as a replacement for other ingredients?*

12 *Underline* **when growing up** *in the question. Now look for mentions of something similar in the text. There are references to childhood, family and kids, but which one is about the author of the cookbook as a child?*

14 *Underline* **pictures** *in the question. Can you find a word with a similar meaning? Are there pictures of every dish?*

Questions 8–14

*Look at the six reviews of cookbooks, **A–F**, on page 27.*

For which are the following statements true?

*Write the correct letter, **A–F**, in boxes 8–14 on your answer sheet.*

NB You may use any letter more than once

8 It has general tips about how to cook.

9 It helps people who are confused by the amount of information online.

10 The recipes are good for people who want to lose weight.

11 The recipes replace standard ingredients with healthier options.

12 Some of the recipes are for dishes the writer ate when growing up.

13 It includes recipes for drinks.

14 It contains pictures of every dish.

What is Reading Passage 2?

- two texts relating to work
- two or three tasks, with a total of 13 questions

What does it test?

- understanding texts that focus on work related issues, e.g. applying for jobs, company policies, pay and conditions, workplace facilities, staff development and training
- the ability to retrieve and provide factual information from authentic texts that might be encountered at work, e.g. staff development and training materials or job descriptions

Task information: *Notes completion*

Notes completion requires you to understand the main points and supporting detail from a text or part of a text.

You have to:
- read the notes and identify what kind of information you need.
- scan the text to find the specific information, using any headings in the notes to help you find the parts you need.
- complete the spaces in the notes by choosing a number, word or words from the text.

Task information: *Sentence completion*

Sentence completion requires you to understand specific information from a text or part of a text.

You have to:
- read the sentences and identify the parts of the text to which they refer.
- find a number, word or words from the text which fit in the space and copy them into the space.

1 **Read the text below. What is it about?**

a performing on stage at a festival

b attending a festival outdoors

c getting a job helping at a festival

Working at an outdoor music festival

If you'd like to see some world-class acts for free and you're not afraid of hard work, consider getting a job at a music festival. From working as a security guard to cleaning or serving food, there are many positions to be filled. However, work at the most popular festivals is highly sought-after, so consider becoming a volunteer. It might lead to more, but if not, at least you will be entertained and meet interesting people.

With outdoor work, be prepared for anything in terms of weather as big festivals are very seldom cancelled. Contrary to what many people think, there is very little chance of running into famous musicians in the backstage area. They tend to retreat to their trailers to avoid the crowds. But as a festival worker, you'll meet many interesting people all day and night.

2 **Complete the sentences below.**

Choose **ONE WORD ONLY** from the text for each answer.

1 What is the maximum number of words you may put in a space?

2 Now, underline the key information in the sentences below. What kind of word do you expect to see in the space (e.g. noun, adjective, verb)?

   1 Starting as a .... is a good way to get work at a festival.

   2 You must be ready to work in all ....

   3 Celebrities generally spend most of their time in .... when they are not performing.

3 **Now look at the text and underline where you find the answers.**

You should spend about 20 minutes on **Questions 15–27**, which are based on the two reading texts below.

Read the text below and answer **Questions 15–21**.

Dupont Mortgage Brokers: an eco-friendly workplace

Here at Dupont, we take our responsibility to the environment seriously. We are committed to considering sustainability issues when making decisions about planning and management. We aim to improve environmental performance by continually addressing environmental risk. To this end we have established a dedicated team to promote environmental awareness and ensure employees are aware of their environmental responsibilities. We encourage all employees to notify us when they see that company practices have a negative impact on the environment and need improvement.

We have done a lot in the last years to be greener in our workplace, but we could do more. Here's a reminder of some basic actions that will lessen our environmental impact:

Good habits in the office

We ask that all employees continue to turn off all lights and electronic equipment, including computers, at the end of the day. If this isn't done, we are asking 'offenders' to pay a small fine – there is a jar for this purpose on Kevin Wu's desk and the proceeds will go to the *Positive Planet* regeneration scheme.

We're doing our bit to reduce landfill by having our used ink cartridges collected. These should be placed in the box by the stationery cupboard - Jetco, the manufacturer we use, arranges collection for recycling on a monthly basis.

In terms of reducing our use of paper, first consider whether it's necessary to print out a document. Will a soft copy do? Save it on file and save paper! We've ordered good quality recycled paper for the office to be used as needed; where you do have to print, make use of both sides of the paper. There is a tub in the photocopying room for any used paper; the cleaners will empty this into the large bin for recycling every week.

Placing orders

In terms of ordering stationery and office equipment, please use the following approved suppliers, which are all committed to reducing waste and eliminating their carbon footprint:

GreenCo Office Supplies

Down to Earth

Jetco

Okapi Stationery

In all parts of the company including office, kitchen, bathrooms and staffroom, please use 'green' products, provided that they are within the allocated budget. To check a product's rating in terms of environmental impact, go to checkisitgreen.co.uk and opt for products that have a four-star rating or higher.

Action plan for *Note completion*

1 Look at the title and any headings and decide what the text is about.

2 Read the text very quickly to get a general idea of its structure and ideas.

3 Read the question and see how many words you must write for each space.

4 Read the notes carefully and underline important words.

5 Find the part of the text which contains the same information as the notes.

6 Read the relevant part of the text carefully and underline the word that you think fits in the space.

 TIP Use the headings in the notes to help you find the part of the text you need.

 TIP When you look at the numbered space, try to predict what kind of information is required. Is it a noun, verb or adjective? Is it a number, date or name?

TIP Write the word exactly as it appears in the text. You will not have to make any changes to the word. Check if it is singular or plural.

Advice

Look at how the notes are structured. In this case, the headings in the notes are not exactly the same as the headings in the text but they lead you through the text in order.

15 *Which word in the first paragraph of the text means* **set up** *as in the notes? You'll notice this word is followed by two words in the text – how many words are you allowed to put in the space?*

18 *Recycling is mentioned in relation to two kinds of office supply. Which one of these is picked up by the supplier?*

20 *The notes mention a list, whereas the text does not. However, can you see a list in the text? What are on this list?*

Questions 15–21

Complete the notes below.

*Choose **ONE WORD ONLY** from the text for each answer.*

Dupont, an environmentally sustainable workplace

Commitment to the environment

- ongoing process
- set up a **15** .... to focus on implementing policy
- workers to identify **16** .... that cause harm

In the office

- turn off lights, computers when leaving
- forget to turn off equipment ⟶ put donation in **17** ....
- recycle **18** .... ⟶ current brand organises pick up

Paper

- avoid printing
- use - recycled
     - both sides
- put in **19** .... when discarding

Purchasing

- choose products from a list of **20** ....
- where **21** .... allows, order eco-friendly products
- look up eco-rating

Read the text below and answer Questions 22–27.

Becoming a tour guide
Many people dream of travelling for a living, but what does it actually involve?

Tour guides accompany visitors on tours, providing special information on places of interest, and managing the schedule for the tour.

Starting out

While you can work as a tour guide without formal qualifications, entry to the occupation may be easier if you can show you are qualified and you may like to consider taking a course. Options vary, but the Centre for Further Education offers a *General Certificate in Guiding* along with more specific subjects such as *Guiding a 4WD Tour* and *Guiding a Ski Tour.* You will also get some informal training on the job.

Many would-be guides start out as volunteers, working in a place they know well, showing tourists around. Experience in a related field such as hospitality is generally looked on favourably by employers in the travel industry.

Skills and qualities needed

While everyone brings their own personality to the job, there are some basic qualities that all tour guides should possess:

- Energy and enthusiasm are an absolute must – when the day's tour is done, a guide still needs to study commentary and confirm the next day's activities, so you will often need to operate on very little sleep.

- A friendly personality is needed when interacting with clients, tour operators and the general public.

- An insight into a wide range of cultures helps a guide negotiate all kinds of issues, not only in the place being visited, but also among the people on the tour.

- Knowledge of emergency procedure and the ability to remain calm in a crisis will stand any tour guide in good stead. Your confidence as tour leader will filter down to the group.

- The ability to handle any tricky questions that arise is a crucial component of the role. If you're stuck for an answer, you should be able to find the information and follow up.

Know the reality

Life as a tour guide often requires long spells away from home. Some find that busy times at work fall on holidays they would like to spend with loved ones. Burn-out is also a factor to consider but it does not mean the end of a career in travel. There are often openings for roles in product development and sales within the industry; experience as a guide will stand you in good stead for these.

Action plan for *Sentence completion*

1 Use the title and any headings in the text to decide what the text is about.

2 Read the text very quickly to get a general idea of its structure and ideas.

3 Look at the instructions to see how many words you must write for each space.

4 Read the sentences carefully and underline important words. As you do this, try to predict what kind of words you need for each space (e.g. noun, verb, adjective).

5 Find the part of the text which contains the same information as the sentence.

6 Carefully read the relevant part of the text and mark the word that you think fits in the space.

 TIP The sentences follow the order of the information in the text.

TIP When you have finished, read the sentences through again and ensure they make sense.

Advice

22 *From the question, you can see that the word you need will be plural, as the next word is* **aren't**.

24 *Look at the first bullet point in the text. The question mentions* **a lack of**. *What words in this bullet point reflect this idea?*

27 *Look at the final paragraph, which is about openings for those moving on from being travel guides. Two possibilities are suggested; the question mentions putting together new tours – this is another way of saying* **product development***. What is the other possibility?*

Complete the sentences below.

Choose **NO MORE THAN TWO WORDS** *from the passage for each answer.*

22 ....qualifications.... aren't necessary to become a tour guide but they can help.

23 If you have worked in ....volunteers hospitality...., it may help your chances of employment as a tour guide.

24 Tour guides must be prepared to work despite a lack of ....compensatory.... sleep

25 An understanding of different ....cultures.... will help a tour guide manage groups of people.

26 Dealing with difficult ....questions.... is part of working as a tour guide.

27 Being a tour guide may lead to a position in ....industry.... or in putting together new tours for customers.

(product)

What is Reading Passage 3?

- a text of up to 900 words, usually factual or descriptive, from a wide range of contexts, e.g. from a newspaper, magazine or book
- two or three tasks, with a total of 13 questions
- a longer and usually slightly more challenging text than Passages 1 and 2

What does it test?

- understanding extended prose with an emphasis on descriptive and instructive, rather than argumentative, texts
- a range of reading skills including reading for main ideas and detail as well as understanding the structure of a text at a sentence and paragraph level

Task information: *Matching headings*

Matching headings requires you to understand the main point of each paragraph or section in the text.

You have to:
- read the headings, identified with lower-case Roman numerals, which refer to the main point of each paragraph or section. A second may comprise two or more paragraphs but will be labelled as one section, requiring a single heading.
- find which paragraph or section contains the information in each heading. Remember there may be more headings than you need.

Task information: *Multiple-choice*

Multiple-choice requires both general and detailed understanding of the text.

You have to:
- read questions or incomplete statements which focus on the ideas and information in the text. The questions are in the same order as the information in the text. They may refer to a small part of the text or a long section of it. Occasionally, the last question may refer to the text as a whole.
- choose the correct options **A, B, C** or **D** to answer the question or complete the statement so that it means the same as the text. There is never more than one correct option in a *4-option multiple-choice* task.

Task information: *Summary completion*

Summary completion requires you to understand the main points and supporting detail from a text or part of a text.

You have to:
- read the summary and the part(s) of the text to which it refers. The information may not be in the same order as in the text.
- complete the spaces in the notes by choosing a number, word or words from the text.

1 Read the text quickly to see what it is about.

Fjaðrárgljúfur Canyon, in Iceland, is little known and is so far not as crowded as many other sites of natural beauty in the area, such as Jökulsárlón glacier lagoon. Its tranquility and isolation mean that it is an ideal location for photographers and hikers alike.

While the valley itself was relatively recently formed, just after the last ice age approximately 10,000 years ago, the bedrock here is significantly older, said to date back two million years. The ravine was created as the runoff from a glacial lake wore away the soft stone, leaving only the harder rocks remaining.

2 What would be the best heading for this text?

  a An unspoiled area

  b An ancient valley

  c A popular attraction

3 When you have chosen the heading you think is correct, look at the other two headings; why are they unsuitable?

You should spend about 20 minutes on **Questions 28–40**, which are based on Reading Passage 3 on pages 39–40.

Questions 28–32

*The text has five sections, **A–E**.*

Choose the correct heading for each paragraph, **A–E**, from the list of headings below.

Write the correct number, **i–vii**, in boxes 28–32 on your answer sheet.

28 Paragraph A *i*

29 Paragraph B *vii*

30 Paragraph C *iii*

31 Paragraph D *ii*

32 Paragraph E *vi*

List of Headings

   i Preserving the beauty of the area

   ii Getting from one side to the other

   iii When the Falls stopped flowing

   iv Permanent damage to the bottom of the river

   v The involvement of two countries

   vi Physical characteristics of the Falls

   vii Depictions of the Falls

Action plan for *Matching headings*

1 If there is a *Matching headings* task, it comes before the text. This is to encourage you to read the headings before you read the text.

2 Check how many headings there are and how many paragraphs / sections in the text.

3 Read the first paragraph of the text quickly. Underline the main ideas and choose the best heading.

4 Do the same for the remaining paragraphs. You can only use each heading once.

5 There will be more headings than you need. Read the one(s) you haven't used and check that it can't go in any of the paragraphs / sections.

TIP If you are not sure about one of the paragraphs, go back when you have done the rest of the task and you haven't got so many headings to choose from.

TIP The headings are about the main ideas in the paragraphs / sections, not one or two details.

Advice

28 *Which nations are the Falls situated in? Who controls the flow of water?*

31 *Section D is about bridges and boats; what is the function of bridges and boats? Which heading best reflects this function?*

Niagara Falls

The Niagara Falls, on the Niagara River on the border between Ontario, Canada, and New York state, US, are one of North America's most famous spectacles.

A

The Falls are in two main parts, separated by Goat Island. The larger part, on the Canadian bank, is Horseshoe Falls; its height is 185 feet and the length of its curving crest line is about 2,200 feet. The American Falls, adjoining the right bank in the US, are 190 feet high and 1,060 feet wide.

The water that runs over the falls comes from the Great Lakes. Ninety percent of the water goes over the Horseshoe Falls. Originally, as much as 5.5 billion gallons of water per hour went over the Falls and, from 1842 to 1905, the site of the Falls receded upstream at an average rate of about 5.5 feet per year. Today the amount is controlled by the Canadian and American governments to slow erosion.

B

The first known image of Niagara Falls is an engraving by an unidentified Dutch printmaker which was first published in 1697 in a book by Father Louis Hennepin, a priest accompanying a French expedition to America. Alongside the engraving, Hennepin provided a description of the Falls, suggesting it to be over six hundred feet tall, and audible fifteen leagues away (a distance that could be the equivalent of a 15-hour walk). This turned out to be a wild exaggeration as the Falls in fact rise 170 feet. However, as the first European reporter to have seen the Falls, Hennepin's description is significant for the fact that it dominated the collective imagination of the Falls in the century to come.

C

In 1848, for the first time in recorded history, the falls ran dry. The river bed started drying quickly, leaving fish and turtles floundering. People came from miles around to explore the riverbed; they found things that had been hidden for years such as artefacts of the War of 1812. This phenomenon occurred due to strong westerly winds keeping water in Lake Erie, along with an ice jam that dammed the river near Buffalo, New York. Below the Falls, workers were able to head out onto the riverbed and clear away rocks which had been a navigation hazard to the steamboat, Maid of the Mist. It is estimated that the river stopped for 30–40 hours in total.

Later, in 1969, the US Army Corps of Engineers built a series of dams which brought the water flow over the American Falls to a small trickle. This was in order to enable a study of the rock formations at the crest of the Falls and see whether there was any way to remove the rock at the base of the American Falls. In the end, the engineers decided to let nature take its course.

D

Engineer Charles Ellet completed the first bridge across the Falls in 1948. Seven years later John Roebling oversaw construction of another suspension bridge, this one with two levels: one for carriages and the other for locomotive traffic, allowing the Grand Trunk Railway to connect from Canada to the USA. Before it was built, there was widespread doubt that a suspension bridge would be able to bear the weight of a locomotive; no bridge of this kind had ever done this. Roebling's bridge cost $450,000 and became one of the world's most famous bridges.

Another famous attraction in Niagara Falls is the steamboat, the *Maid of the Mist*. This boat made its maiden voyage in 1846 as a ferry, charging to transport people, cargo, and mail across the river. Before that, rowboats took people who needed to get across the Niagara river below the Falls. However, when Ellet's newly constructed bridge began to diminish its business in 1848, the *Maid of the Mist* concentrated on sightseeing and took visitors very close to the Horseshoe Falls. Several boats have taken the title *Maid of the Mist* since then, and to this day, *Maid of the Mist VI* and *Maid of the Mist VII* operate and since 2013 have been leaving from the US side of the Falls only. At 74 ft and 80 ft respectively, these boats are able to carry 600 visitors a piece, right to the base of the Falls.

E

It is often asked why the water of the Niagara Falls seems to take on an aquamarine colour, which is especially intense on sunny days. The reason is that the oxygen and mineral rich waters provide a conducive environment for the growth of algae called diatoms. The bodies of diatoms behave like prisms, reflecting a sparkling aquamarine. Minerals also contribute to the water's colour; dissolved limestone, shale and sandstone form salts that tint the river, while clean and well-oxygenated water helps this effect show through.

The foam in the water at the base of the Falls is not a man-made phenomenon. It is actually calcium carbonate from the mist as it evaporates while going over the Falls. This mixes with decaying diatoms and other algae to produce the foam. Moving further downstream, it remixes with the water and disappears. While in the 1950s and 1960s there was scum from phosphates and other pollutants, this is not the case today.

Action plan for *Multiple-choice*

1   If the *Multiple-choice* questions are the first task for a text, read the text quickly first to get an idea of the general structure and information in the text.

2   Read each question or incomplete statement and the options A–D.

3   Scan the text to find the part of the text you need and read for more detail to find the answer.

4   Reread all options again and choose the one you believe to be correct.

 TIP Be careful – the incorrect options may use similar wording or synonyms for what is in the text but they will be clearly wrong. There is only one correct answer.

 TIP These questions will follow the order of the text.

 TIP Do not answer the questions by using your general knowledge – you have to find the information in the text.

Questions 33–36

*Choose the correct letter, **A**, **B**, **C** or **D**.*

Write the correct letter in boxes 33–36 on your answer sheet.

33 Hennepin's account of his visit to Niagara Falls

    A   understated the scale of the Falls.

    B   influenced many people's impression of the Falls.

    C   conflicted with the illustration that accompanied it.

    D   attracted criticism from locals at the time it was written.

34 What caused the event that happened at the Falls in 1848?

    A   A transport company was able to assess the volume of water.

    B   The tourist industry took action in order to attract more people.

    C   A natural phenomenon caused the source of the falls to be blocked.

    D   Engineers held back the falls in order to complete their research.

35 Roebling's bridge was remarkable because

    A   it consisted of two separate levels.

    B   it was inexpensive for a bridge of its kind.

    C   it was the first bridge built across the Niagara Falls.

    D   it was the first bridge of its kind to carry a train.

36 What causes the water of the Falls to be foamy?

    A   A combination of naturally-occurring substances.

    B   The pressure of dropping from a height.

    C   A problem further up the river.

    D   Pollution from industry.

Advice

Use distinctive information in the incomplete statement / question to help you find the relevant part of the text: Look for 'Hennepin' (33), '1948' (34) etc.

33 *Check each of these options against the text, e.g. did Hennepin say the Falls were larger or smaller than they really were?; Why was Hennepin's account significant?*

34 *The question asks, 'What caused...'. A transport company, tourists and engineer are all mentioned in this section of text but the key words are 'occurred due to...'*

36 *Note that an option may be mentioned in the text but if you read further, you can discount it (e.g. 'this is not the case today').*

Action plan for *Summary completion*

1 If the *Summary completion* is the first task for a text, read the text quickly first to get an idea of the general structure and information in the text.

2 Look at the instructions to see how many words you must write for each space.

3 Read the summary carefully and underline important words. As you do this try to predict what kind of words you need for each space (e.g. noun, verb, adjective).

4 Find the part of the text which contains the same information as the summary.

TIP Use the heading of the summary to help you find the information in the text.
Carefully read the relevant part of the text and underline the words that you think fit in the spaces.

TIP The information you need will normally be in one part of the passage. Remember the spaces may not be in the same order as the information in the text.

TIP When you have finished, read the summary through and check it makes sense.

Advice

*Look at the title of the summary. Now find the part of the text that is about the **Maid of the Mist**.*

37 *The first space is about what happened before the **Maid of the Mist**. Can you find a word in the text that means before?*

40 *The final space relates to passenger capacity. What sort of information do you expect to find in the space?*

Questions 37–40

Complete the summary below.

*Choose **ONE WORD ONLY** from the passage for each answer.*

Write your answers in boxes 37–40 on your answer sheet.

The Maid of the Mist

Prior to the *Maid of the Mist's* first voyage, people used **37** ....Ferry.... [Steamboat] to get across the Niagara River at the base of the Falls. When launched in 1946, the steamboat carried **38** ....mail.... and cargo as well as passengers but after a suspension bridge was built, the main purpose of the *Maid of the Mist* was for **39** ...sightseeing... The original steamboat has been replaced many times and two *Maids of the Mist* currently run: *Maid of the Mist VI* and *VII*, which each have a passenger capacity of **40** ....600.... Exhibition

---

What is Writing Task 1?

- a writing task which requires you to respond to a situation by writing a letter, for example asking for information or explaining something

What does it test?

- presenting a clear purpose in the letter
- using a tone that is appropriate for the task
- showing a range of accurate grammar and punctuation
- using appropriate vocabulary and spelling
- organising your thoughts and ideas clearly

Task information

This task requires you to write a letter in response to information given in the task.

You have to:

- read the first sentence(s) to get an idea of what the situation is and who you are writing to.
- include the three points that are required in the task.
- plan, write and check your work in 20 minutes.
- set your writing out in the form of a letter.

STRATEGIES

Before you write

A Reading the question

Read the task below and think about the questions in boxes 1–5. This is the kind of task you will see in Writing Task 1.

1 Read the question carefully. What does the first sentence tell you?

2 Read the next part of the task. Who will you have to write to? What tone will it be (formal / neutral / informal)?

5 What is a polite way to ask about the cost?

Writing Task 1

You should spend about 20 minutes on this task.

You work for a small company. Your manager has asked you to arrange a party in a restaurant for everyone from your workplace.

Write a letter to the owner of a restaurant. In the letter:

- *give the reason for the party and details of when you would like to go to the restaurant*
- *describe what food the group will require*
- *say how many people will attend and ask how much it will cost*

Write at least 150 words.

You do **NOT** need to write any addresses.

Begin your letter as follows:

Dear ....,

3 What is the reason for the party? What kind of details would the restaurant need to know?

4 What will the restaurant need to know about the types of food the group would like?

B Understanding the task

Read the sentences below about the task on the previous page. Which of them are True (✓) and which are False (✗)?

1 You should write to your manager.
2 You can make changes to suit your real workplace (e.g. ask about a party that is just for one department).
3 You should know a lot about different kinds of food to answer the second point.
4 You only need to write briefly about the reason for the party.
5 You need to cover all the bullet points.
6 You should use bullet points in your answer.

C Selecting from the task

Look again at the task on page 43. Underline or highlight the most important parts of the task.

Now look at the expressions / sentences below to start your letter and say which you could use for this task. If it is not appropriate, think about why.

Dear Mr Smith,

Dear Owner,

Dear Sir or Madam,

Dear Betty,

How should you begin a letter to   – someone whose name you do not know?

– someone whose name you know but you have never met or you do not know well?

– someone who you know, but not well?

– someone at work with whom you have a lot of contact?

– a personal friend?

D Writing the letter

When you have looked carefully at the task and planned what you are going to write, you are ready to write your letter. Use the words in the box to fill the spaces in the sample answer below.

booking	main purpose	much appreciated	options
	questions	terms of	total cost

Dear Sir or Madam,

I work for TFD Insurance and am writing to inquire about making a **1** .... at your restaurant for a company party. There are 25 of us and we would like to come at 7 p.m. on June 6.

The **2** .... of the event is to thank the employees for their work and we will be presenting some awards to staff members at the end. It would be perfect if we could reserve the private dining room for this. In **3** .... the food that we require, we are interested in Banquet Option B from your menu, with dessert and coffee, as it provides a lot of variety and caters well for vegetarian guests. I see that there are also gluten-free **4** .... which we would like to order in advance for four people.

It would be **5** .... if you could provide us with a quote for the **6** .... of the banquet and room hire for 25 people and, also, if you could let me know if we can make a reservation for 6 June.

If you have any **7** .... in relation to this, please do not hesitate to contact me.

Yours faithfully,
Melanie Wilson

After you write

E Checking your answer

Read the answer at the top of page 46 as if you were checking your own work in the test. Decide whether the candidate has completed the task satisfactorily.

1   There is one spelling error. Can you find it?

2   Now correct the errors.

   a   Correct the errors that have been highlighted.

   b   Fill the marked space 5 with a suitable word.

   c   Suggest another word to use instead of repeating 'group' every time.

Dear Jimmy's Pizzeria,

I am writing to book a table for a celebration for my workmates. We will be having our fifth birthday as a company and have decided to bring all of the **1** staffs out for dinner. We would like to come on the 17th of August and we will be a group of 40 people.
2 You have got room for that many people in your restaurant?

If possible, we'd like a variety of pizzas, including some for our **3** vegetarians employees. We'd also like to order salad and bread to share and your tiramisu dessert to finish. Perhaps you can advise me about how many **4** pizza we will need as I have never made a booking for a group of this size before.

I would be **5** .... if you could give us an estimate of how much this will cost and also let me know wether it is possible to book for a group of 40 from 6 p.m. on the 17th of August.

Please call me if you need more **6** informations.

Kind regards,
Jared Poole

Some of these errors are habits influenced by the writer's first language.
Can you identify some of your own habitual mistakes?

TIP Make a note of your habitual errors and check for them when you write.

Useful language: asking for information

1 **In the letter, you may need to ask for information. Match the expressions (1–4) with the answers (a–d) and then put them in order from most formal to least formal.**

    1 I am writing to enquire

    2 I would be grateful if you could provide

    3 I just wanted to ask if

    4 Could you also let me know

        a you know what time the party starts.

        b about the possibility of reserving a place on the course.

        c details of any previous experience you have had as a nanny.

        d what time everyone will be showing up?

2 **What mistake has this IELTS candidate made?**

I would appreciate if you could send me details of your prices.

3 **Without looking back at the sample answer in Section D, fill the spaces. Then check your answers.**

It would be appreciated if you could **a** .... us with a quote for the total cost of the banquet and room hire for 25 people and also if you could **b** .... if we can make a reservation for 6 June.

4 **Choose the correct word or phrase in italics in these sentences.**

    1 I *would / will* like to know if you have facilities for children as we will be bringing our three-year-old with us.

    2 I was wondering if you could *give me information / let me know* how much the set menu costs.

    3 Could you *provide us / give us* with a list of the people who will be attending the event?

    4 We wanted to *request / enquire* about renting a flat that you have advertised.

    5 It would be *grateful / appreciated* if you could send me details of the menu.

Useful language: synonyms

In order to avoid repeating the same words in your writing, it is a good idea to use synonyms (e.g. in the letter on page 46 – *The main purpose of the event is to thank the* employees *for their work and we will be presenting some awards to* staff members *at the end*). To avoid repeating *employees*, *staff members* is used.

1 **Look at the following sentences and think of alternative words, to avoid repetition.**

  1 There is a problem with the heating in our home. The heating on the upper level of our home does not work at all.

  2 I'm writing to enquire about the position of camp leader. I believe I am very well-suited to the position.

  3 I'm sorry I accidentally damaged your speaker set while I was looking after your flat. I didn't notice I had damaged it until I tried to use it the following day.

  4 You should bring that dish to the barbecue because everyone loves that dish.

  5 I am writing to request three weeks off at the end of winter. I am requesting time off then because it will not be a busy time in the office.

  6 Where are the supplies we will need to set up the festival? I will need those supplies when I arrive, so I can have everything ready for 10 a.m.

In the IELTS exam, it is important not to spend more than 20 minutes on Task 1 so that you have enough time for Task 2, which is longer and worth more marks.

Action plan for *A letter for work purposes*

When practising, you may need to spend more than 20 minutes at first. Record how long you take to do the task and every time you practise, try to reduce the time until you can do Task 1 in 20 minutes.

Before you write

This action plan takes you through writing a letter.

1 Read the task carefully. Think about what the first statement tells you.

2 Look at the bullet points and make sure you are clear what you have to cover in your letter.

3 Make notes on anything you want to include in the letter:

Dear … Would you know the person's name? Would you use their first name or Mr / Ms / Mrs?	
Bullet point 1	
Bullet point 2	
Bullet point 3	
What is the appropriate way to end your letter in this situation?	

4 Write your letter. Does the situation mean that it should be formal, neutral or informal? Remember the main purpose of the letter. You must base your writing on ideas in the task, but you will lose marks if you copy the text word for word.

After you write

5 Read through your letter.

Check for

content – is the purpose of the letter clear? Have you covered the necessary points?

tone – is the letter formal / neutral / informal? Is it polite?

grammar – do your verbs agree with their subjects? Have you used prepositions correctly? Have you used articles correctly?

spelling – if you have copied any words, have you copied them correctly? Have you avoided the mistakes you commonly make?

length – have you written 150 words?

6 Correct any mistakes you find but do not rewrite the whole letter.

Writing Task 1

You should spend about 20 minutes on this task.

You work for a company. You have seen some information online about a training course that would be useful for your work.
Write a letter to your manager. In the letter:

- **give details of the course**
- **say how the course would be useful**
- **explain how the company could help you do this course.**

Write at least 150 words.

Advice

Remember, you will not get extra points if you write more than 150 words but you will lose marks if you write less.

Do not include extra information that is not mentioned in the instructions. Instead, develop the ideas in the instructions.

What is Writing Task 2?

- an agree / disagree essay

What does it test?

- expressing and evaluating ideas
- use of an appropriate style
- grammar and punctuation
- vocabulary and spelling
- organisation and paragraphing

Task information

This task requires you to present an argument in a clear and well-organised way.

You have to:

- write at least 250 words in 40 minutes.
- discuss the idea expressed in the task.
- give your opinion and support it with relevant examples.
- conclude with a brief statement of your opinion.

STRATEGIES

Before you write

A   Reading the question

Read the task below and think about the questions in the boxes. This is the kind of task you will see in Writing Task 2.

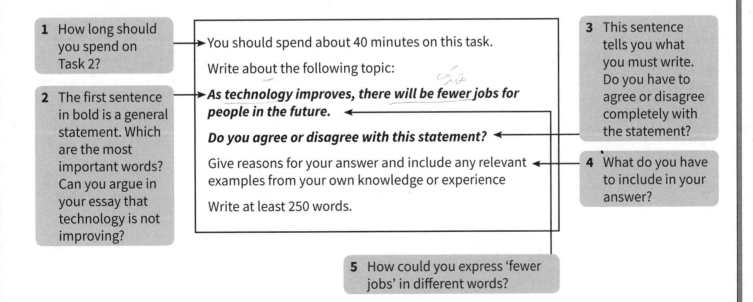

1 How long should you spend on Task 2?

You should spend about 40 minutes on this task.

Write about the following topic:

2 The first sentence in bold is a general statement. Which are the most important words? Can you argue in your essay that technology is not improving?

As technology improves, there will be fewer jobs for people in the future.

Do you agree or disagree with this statement?

Give reasons for your answer and include any relevant examples from your own knowledge or experience

Write at least 250 words.

3 This sentence tells you what you must write. Do you have to agree or disagree completely with the statement?

4 What do you have to include in your answer?

5 How could you express 'fewer jobs' in different words?

B   Planning your answer

Before you begin your essay, it is important to plan what you want to say and how you want to organise it. This is one way of presenting your answer for an agree / disagree essay:

Stage 1	An **introduction** paraphrasing the first part of the task and saying what your position is going to be.
Stage 2	Explain to what **extent you agree**.
Stage 3	Explain to what **extent you disagree**.
Stage 4	Give your final **conclusion**.

Match these notes for Writing Task 2 on page 51 with Stages 1–4.

a *some jobs still need people / new jobs created*

....

b *lots of tech advances – more in future: positive and negative for jobs*

....

c *new positions needed – technicians, creative – the arts*

....

d *car industry – losing jobs, 3D-printing, drivers, robots*

....

C Developing a clearly structured argument

👁 Using the right words in phrases to link your ideas together gives your writing coherence and makes your essay easy to follow.

1 **Read this sample answer and fill spaces 1–4 with expressions a–d and spaces 5–8 with expressions e–h.**

The world has already seen incredible technological advances and it seems that progress in the areas of robotics and artificial intelligence is not slowing down. **1** .... this will prove to be the end of some jobs, this essay will argue that it will open up opportunities in other fields.

It is true that many jobs that require manual labour may not exist in the future. We only need to look at the automotive industry and the vast cuts that have already been made there in terms of labour. In the future, this will only continue. **2** .... advancements like 3D printing may affect sectors such as manufacturing and construction; driverless vehicles will mean that we don't need taxi drivers or bus drivers; many dirty and dangerous jobs that are now done by humans may one day be done by robots.

3 .... other positions may be created by these changes. Humans may still be needed to maintain, service and repair machines, **4** .... until robots are able to do these tasks themselves. The job of inventing and designing, along with project management will also likely still be done by people. There will always be a demand for humans in sectors that require empathy, such as childcare and teaching. In many other areas, like medicine, professionals may use technological advances in their work **5** .... the human component will still be needed. Art and literature are other fields where it is hard to imagine machines taking over.

6 .... it seems that some types of job will suffer when technological progress gets to a certain point. **7** .... some human roles will remain and other employment opportunities will appear **8** .... the advances.

---

    a at least

    b While

    c However

    d For example

    e as a result of

    f but

    g On the other hand

    h Overall

Useful language: style

1 Compare the language of A and B below. Which style is more suitable for an essay?

> **A**
>
> I reckon robots will take over people's jobs. But it won't be that bad because there will also be some new jobs, like fixing the robots – it's not as bad as we think.

> **B**
>
> To my mind, humans will increasingly be replaced by robots in certain roles. However, other new types of employment may appear, for instance working in robotics as a technician, which may mean that the outlook is more hopeful than some anticipate.

2 Here are some language features of A. Can you find examples of them?
1 informal verb
2 using a dash (–) instead of a linking word
3 repeating vocabulary
4 simple vocabulary
5 a conjunction / linking word at the beginning of a sentence

3 Now look at B. Can you find examples of these language features?
1 passive verb
2 neutral / formal vocabulary
3 a relative pronoun
4 a modal verb
5 an adverb at the beginning of a sentence

4 Choose the most appropriate phrases in italics for use in an essay from these sentences.
1 *You can't say / Few would argue* that robots can do everything that humans do.
2 *I think / In my view*, the medical profession will always need human workers.
3 There are *heaps of / numerous* jobs that can be done more efficiently by machines.

Useful language: impersonal structures

1   Explain the meaning of these impersonal phrases.

It is widely believed that…

It is unfortunate that…

It is beyond doubt that…

It is frequently argued that…

It is well established that…

It is occasionally the case that…

It is sometimes assumed that…

2   **Now make sentences with the phrases in Exercise 2 above, using the ideas in this box, or your own.**

> Tourism / The economy
>
> Recycling / Environment
>
> Money / Happiness
>
> Preparation / Success

Example:

It is well established that *tourism has a positive effect on the economy of many countries in the region.*

Useful language: paragraphing

⊙ **Read the following essay. It is a good response to the task. However, it does not have paragraphs, which will lose marks. Mark each place where you think a new paragraph should start and write 'new para' in the margin. Explain your decision.**

IELTS candidate's essay

Computers and robotics are revolutionising the way work is done and already many industries are using machines for work that was formerly done by humans. It seems that, with a few exceptions, this trend will continue and the majority of jobs that exist now will no longer exist in the future. There is certainly a case to be made that some types of work require the human touch. It is difficult to imagine areas such as childcare and counselling not being staffed by people as the human component seems so vital. It is also hard to envisage a time when people will not want to work, as many get a lot of meaning from their jobs and have an entrepreneurial spirit. These people will always find a job to do, to create something new or to make money. This being said, it cannot be denied that technological progress means that huge numbers of the world's workers who do manual labour may find themselves out of work. Automation and new processes for design and manufacturing are making many jobs disappear. There has been talk of a 'living wage', presumably paid by taxes from those who earn money to people whose jobs will no longer be needed in society. That may not happen for many years but it could well be that the world is heading in that direction. On the whole, it would appear that although there are a few jobs that will always require people, employment as we know it will change drastically if technology continues to improve. A great deal of the work that is now done by people, will be achieved either by machines or by a smaller number of people than currently do that work.

TIP Do not try to learn sample answers and rewrite them in the exam. Your essay will not fit the task exactly, even if it is about a similar subject. The examiners can recognise a prepared answer and you will lose a lot of marks.

Action plan

Before you write

1 Look at the task and read the question carefully. The task you have to address is printed in **bold italics** but remember to read all the instructions.

2 Underline the important parts of the task.

3 Think about vocabulary and expressions you can use to paraphrase the task and related vocabulary to answer the question.

 TIP Do not copy out the words in the task. You should use your own words.

4 Make notes on the task that you can use as a rough plan.

5 Now write your essay.

After you write

6 Read through your answer. Correct any mistakes clearly and neatly.

7 Check for:

 TIP You will not have time to write a first draft and then a final copy. Just write your essay once.

overall structure – have you addressed all parts of the task?

paragraphing – do you start a new paragraph for each new idea? Have you grouped your ideas logically in paragraphs?

 TIP If you have forgotten to use paragraphs, mark them clearly in the correct place and write 'new para' in the margin.

coherence – have you linked your ideas clearly so it is easy to follow your position?

style – have you used a formal or neutral style of English?

grammar, spelling and **punctuation** – have you started and finished sentences in the right places? Are your verb forms and articles (a / an / the) correct? Have you used capitals, commas and apostrophes correctly?

Writing Task 2

 TIP Allow 5 minutes at the start for planning and another 3-4 minutes at the end for checking.

You should spend about 40 minutes on this task.

Write about the following topic:

Modern technology is used in many workplaces today.

How do you think technology changed the ways people work?

Do you think there any disadvantages of relying on technology at work?

Give reasons for your answer and include any relevant examples from your own knowledge or experience

Write at least 250 words.

TIP For an agree / disagree essay, you do not have to agree or disagree 100% but you should explain clearly in which cases you agree (i.e. to what extent wholly or partially or in certain circumstances).

What is Speaking Part 1?

- a conversation with the examiner lasting 4–5 minutes about two or three everyday topics

Task information

You have to:

- answer questions about yourself, for example about your home, your studies or work, your free time, the things you like and dislike, etc.
- Give full answers – usually in one or two sentences.

What does it test?

- your ability to communicate opinions and information on everyday topics and common experiences or situations

 TIP Try to think in English before you go into the test because this will help you get ready to answer the first questions.

Useful language: study or work

The examiner may start by asking you whether you work or you are a student. He or she will then ask you three questions about your job or your studies.

1   Collect language to talk about the topic.

   Study

   What: Make sure you know the words for the subjects you are studying e.g. biology, business

   Where: Make sure you know the words for the place you are studying e.g. technical college, high school

   Why: Think of words for why you decided to study your subjects e.g. interesting, good career prospects, help in the family business

   How: Think of words to describe what you like about your studies e.g. learning new things, discussing things with my classmates, understanding my subject better

   Work

   What: Make sure you know the words for the job that you do e.g. sales manager, nurse

   Where: Make sure you know the words for the place where you work e.g. car factory, children's hospital

   Why: Think of words for why you decided to do this job e.g. to help people, to get a good salary, to work abroad

   How: Think of words to describe how you feel about your work e.g. satisfying, varied, friendly colleagues

2   **Look at the examiner's questions about work / study on page 63 and answer them using the words and phrases you have collected.**

3   **Collect useful words and phrases to talk about spending time with friends and other topics e.g. hobbies, sports, holidays, languages.**

Useful language: extending your answers

If you answer a question like, 'Do you use computers a lot?' with, 'Yes, I do', the examiner will probably ask you to extend your answer by saying 'Why?' So, it is better to give a longer answer – one or two sentences.

1   **Answer these questions and include a reason or an example.**
    1   Do you use computers a lot?
    2   When did you first learn to use a computer?
    3   What's your favourite kind of film?
    4   How often do you go to the cinema?
    5   Do you like watching sport on television?
    6   Which new sport would you like to try?

2   **It can help you to speak more fluently if you use linking words to join your ideas, rather than speaking in very short sentences. Use these words to join the short sentences below:** *because, but, and, or, although, when, rather than, unless, as well as, while.*
    a   I use a computer every day. I need it for my work. I like to keep in touch with friends on social media.
    b   I learned to use a computer at school. I was six. We did some exercises on it. We enjoyed playing games on it.
    c   I like watching action films. I don't like romantic films. Sometimes action films are too violent.
    d   I'd like to go to the cinema more often. I have a lot of homework.
    e   I don't like watching sport. I watch if there is an international football match.
    f   I'd like to try ice-skating. I am scared of falling over.

3   **Look at the questions about spending time with friends on page 63 and answer them. Remember to give reasons for your answers and use some of the linking words in Exercise 2.**

What is Speaking Part 2?

- a talk lasting 2 minutes

Task information

You have to:

- read about a task that the examiner gives you.
- prepare for 1 minute to give a talk about the task.
- start speaking when the examiner tells you to start.
- stop speaking when the examiner tells you to stop.
- answer one or two questions after your talk.

Useful strategies: preparation time

One minute is a very short time, so it's important to use it well. The examiner will give you some paper and a pencil, so you can make notes if you want. Notes should be short and clear, so you can use them to help you speak.

1   Look at the task on page 63 and decide what item of clothing you want to talk about.

2   Now make a note for each of the four points of the task. Keep each note short – no more than a few words. Don't write in complete sentences. When you have finished, look at the sample notes in the key. Compare your notes with them and decide which would be easier to use.

    Change your notes if necessary.

3   Look at the task on page 63 again and use your notes to give a talk. Make sure you time yourself and try to speak for 2 minutes.

Useful language: clothes and fashion

1   Link the adjectives on the left with the items of clothing on the right by drawing lines between them. Some adjectives go with more than one item of clothing.

checked	flat	floral	full	high-heeled
patterned	plain	round-necked		short-sleeved
long	striped	three-piece	tight	V-necked

cap	dress	jacket	pullover
scarf	shirt	shoes	skirt
suit	trousers		

What does it test?

- your ability to talk for a longer time
- your ability to organise what you say and speak fluently about a personal experience

TIP It is important to choose something that will give you enough to talk about to fill 2 minutes.

TIP It is best to write any notes in English rather than in your own language.

TIP You should talk about all four points of the task, but you don't have to talk about them in the same order as the task. You may have more to say about one or two points than the others.

It is very easy to use simple words like 'good' or 'nice' too much when describing things. Try to use a variety of adjectives.

TIP Try to vary the language you use when you are giving a talk. This will help you to get a higher mark.

2 **What other words can you use to:**

a describe something in a positive way: good, nice, useful

....

b describe something in a negative way: bad, uncomfortable, expensive

....

c describe the way something feels: soft, rough

....

d describe the style of something: smart, old-fashioned

....

e describe the way something makes you feel: comfortable, sad

....

Useful language: giving a talk

1 **It is important to structure your talk well. In particular, you should introduce the topic clearly. Here are some simple ways to start your talk.**

I'm going to tell you about ...
What I want to talk about is ...
I've decided to tell you about ...

2 **Now go back to the notes you made for the task 'My favourite item of clothing'. Give the talk again, but this time record it and time yourself. Try to use some of the language you collected in Exercises 1 and 2.**

TIP You don't have to tell the truth in your talk. You can describe something that didn't happen if you find that easier. Just remember to talk about all the task points.

3 **Listen to your talk and consider how to make it even better.**

- Was there a clear introduction?
- Were all the four task points covered?
- Was the vocabulary varied?
- Were you speaking clearly – too fast or too slowly?
- Were there any grammar mistakes, e.g. 's' missing at the end of he / she verbs?
- Was the talk long enough?

4 **In the next few days, try preparing and giving talks on the topics below.**

Remember to write notes first and then record and time each talk.

- a plan you had to change, why you changed it and what happened
- a film you have seen several times and what you particularly liked about it
- a special meal you had with friends and why you remember it

What is Speaking Part 3?

- a discussion of more general and abstract ideas related to the topic in Part 2 lasting 4–5 minutes

What does it test?

- your ability to use more formal and abstract language and discuss ideas in more depth

Task information

You have to:
- answer questions connected to the topic in Part 2, expressing your opinions and giving reasons for your views.
- answer 3–6 questions.

Useful language: expressing opinions

1   As in Part 2, it is important to use a range of language. It is very easy to introduce opinions by always saying 'I think'. Look at these other ways of introducing opinions.

Personally, I find that …

In my opinion / view …

It seems clear to me that …

I (don't) agree with the idea that …

I'd say that …

2   Practise the expressions above when responding to these questions about stress.

1   What are the best ways to reduce stress?

2   Do you agree that people's lives are more stressful now than in the past?

3   How easy is it to balance work and personal life in today's world?

Useful language: justifying opinions

When you give an opinion, the examiner may ask you to explain why you think that. He or she may also put forward the opposite view and ask for your comments.

Fill in the spaces in the sentences below with these words: *question, evidence, mean, reason, point*

1   I see what you .... but in my view people are expected to work much harder nowadays.

2   In my opinion, feeling happy at work is largely a .... of how supportive your colleagues are.

3   The main .... of the students' campaign is that it costs too much to go to university now.

4   The .... I believe that some courses are becoming too hard is the increasing number of students who drop out of college.

5   There is a lot of .... now that proves people are under pressure.

 TIP The examiner will record the Speaking test. This is for administrative reasons. Don't pay any attention to the recorder, just look at the examiner.

Speaking Part 1

The examiner will start by introducing him / herself and checking your identity. He or she will then ask you some questions about yourself.

Let's talk about what you do. Do you work or are you a student?

Work

- *What's your job?*
- *Why did you choose this kind of work?*
- *What do you like most about your job?*

Study

- *What are you studying?*
- *Why did you choose this subject / these subjects?*
- *What do you like most about your studies?*

TIP The examiner will select either the questions about work or the ones about study depending on your answer to this question

The examiner will then ask you some questions about one or two other topics, for example:

Let's talk about spending time with friends.
1 *When do you spend time with your friends?*
2 *Do you usually go out with friends or spend time with them at home?*
3 *Do you prefer to spend time with a large group of friends or just a few?*
4 *Did you do different things with your friends when you were younger?*

TIP Listen carefully to the questions. Questions 1–3 are about the present, while Question 4 is about the past.

Speaking Part 2

The examiner will give you a topic like the one below and some paper and a pencil.

The examiner will say:

I'm going to give you a topic and I'd like you to talk about it for one to two minutes. Before you talk, you'll have one minute to think about what you're going to say. You can make some notes if you wish.

[1 minute]

All right? Remember you have one to two minutes for this, so don't worry if I stop you. I'll tell you when the time is up. Can you start speaking now, please?

TIP If you don't understand some words on the task, the examiner can say them in a simpler way for you. Just tell the examiner you don't understand. You won't lose marks for this.

> **Describe your favourite item of clothing**
> **You should say:**
> > **what the item of clothing is**
> > **what it looks like**
> > **when and where you got this item of clothing**
> > **and explain why this is your favourite item of clothing.**

TIP Don't worry if you are still speaking when the examiner tells you to stop. It's better to speak right up to the 2-minute limit than to speak for 90 seconds.

TIP The examiner will give marks across all three parts of the test, not a separate mark for each part.

The examiner may ask one or two rounding off questions when you have finished your talk, for example:

- *Do you enjoy shopping for clothes?*

Speaking Part 3

The examiner will ask some general questions which are connected to the topic in Part 2, for example:

We've been talking about your favourite item of clothing. I'd like to discuss with you one or two more general questions relating to this. First, let's consider different types of clothes.

- *What kinds of clothes do young people like to wear in your country?*

Let's talk about shopping habits now.

- *Will people continue to shop in small shops and markets in the future?*

Finally, let's talk about the fashion industry.

- *What contribution does the fashion industry make to a country's economy and reputation?*

Review

1 How many speakers will you hear?
2 Does each task in this part have the same number of questions?
3 What kind of information do you have to listen for in Part 1?
4 Do you have to write the exact words you hear?
5 Is spelling important in Part 1?

Now follow the Action plan reminder on page 65

Useful strategy: deciding what kind of information to write in the spaces

It is very important to look at the words around each space in the notes or form. These words will help you predict the type of information you are looking for.

1   Look at this set of notes. Underline the important information around each space. What does this tell you about the missing information? Try to predict possible answers. The first one has been done for you as an example.

Write **ONE WORD ONLY** for each answer.

Accommodation at Sunnyside Holiday Park

Motel rooms
- $205; sleep 2 people
- all rooms have a view of the
  1 ....

Studios
- $155; sleep 4 people
- no kitchen but a kettle and
  2 ....
  for making drinks and snacks

Budget units
- $222; sleep 4 people
- kitchen with a fridge and
  3 ....
- need to bring your own
  4 ....

Other facilities
- laundry
- games room for all ages
- a **5** .... for
  guests under 12

Advice

Example: a view of

- *so, the answer must be something that is nice to look at*

- *possible answers: lake, sea, river, city, etc.*

🎧 **2** Now listen and complete the information.

11

Useful vocabulary: accommodation registration forms

Look at the completed guest registration form. Complete the spaces using words from the box.

Country
Date and Place of Birth
Date of Issue   Departure Date
Expiry Date   Home Address
Nationality   Postcode
Room No.   Street
Surname   Title

Guest Registration Form

1 .... Ms   **2** .... Rousseau   **First Name** Angelique

Arrival Date 6 April   **3** .... 8 April   **4** 1016

Credit Card   **Credit Card Number**   **5** 05.19
DigiCard   XXXX XXXX XXXX XXXX

Business Address ☒   **6** .... ✓   **City**   Paris

7 ....   **8** 70115   **E-mail**
12 Rue de la Parc   a.rouss eau17@exposte.com

9 .... France   **Telephone** 01 83 77 29 54   **Passport Number**
                                                             224674429

10 ....   **11** .... French   **12** 7.9.2017
18.3.1999   Lyon

Action plan reminder for *Table, note and form completion*

1   How do you know how many words to write?
2   Do you have time to look at the task before you hear the recording?
3   What can you learn from the words around the space?
4   How do you know the topic?

Questions 1–5

Complete the notes below.

*Write **NO MORE THAN ONE WORD** for each answer.*

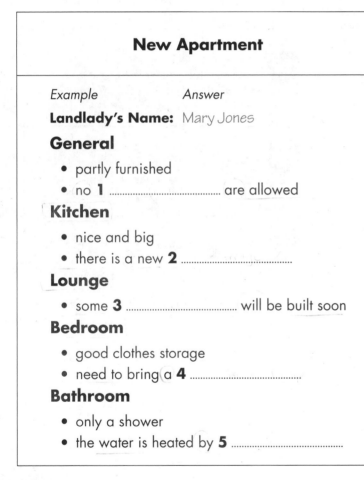

New Apartment

Example	Answer
Landlady's Name:	Mary Jones

General

- partly furnished
- no **1** .... are allowed

Kitchen

- nice and big
- there is a new **2** ....

Lounge

- some **3** .... will be built soon

Bedroom

- good clothes storage
- need to bring a **4** ....

Bathroom

- only a shower
- the water is heated by **5** ....

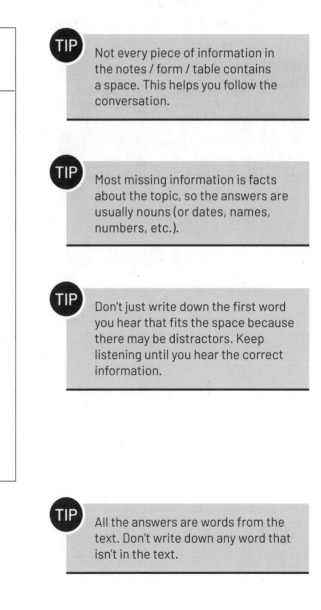

TIP Not every piece of information in the notes / form / table contains a space. This helps you follow the conversation.

TIP Most missing information is facts about the topic, so the answers are usually nouns (or dates, names, numbers, etc.).

TIP Don't just write down the first word you hear that fits the space because there may be distractors. Keep listening until you hear the correct information.

TIP All the answers are words from the text. Don't write down any word that isn't in the text.

Advice

1 Think of synonyms for **allowed**.

2 The word **new** is important here – listen for distraction.

3 This must be something that can be **built** – not just something that will happen in the future.

Questions 6–10

12 *Complete the form below.*

Write **ONE WORD AND / OR A NUMBER** for each answer.

Tenancy Form

Tenant details
- Full name: Andrew **6** ....
- Best contact: **7** andrew171@ .... .com
- Driver's licence: **8** ....

Tenancy details
- Moving-in date: **9** ....
- Rent per week: $315
- **Bond paid**: 10 $ ....

Advice

6 *Look out for letters that are easily confused, such as* **m** *and* **n**, **b** *and* **t**, *etc.*

8 *Some* **numbers** *are actually a mixture of letters and numbers!*

 TIP Be careful not to write down any information that is already given in the form / notes / table, e.g. **$** or **a** or **the**, etc.

TIP Use the subheadings in the form / notes / table to help you follow the conversation and predict what you will hear next.

TIP Make sure your answer fits the grammar around the space, e.g. is the missing word singular or plural?

Review

1 How many speakers will you hear in this part?
2 How many tasks are there usually?
3 Does each task have the same number of questions?
4 What is the speaker's purpose in this part?

Now follow the Action plan reminder on page 68

Useful vocabulary: entertainment

1 Which answer (A, B or C) best fits each space?

1 The whole family enjoyed seeing the acrobats and clowns when the .... came to town.

   A zoo   B amusement park   C circus

2 In my view, Paul Fernley is one of the finest .... of his generation. He's the star of every movie he appears in, even if it's only a minor part.

   A directors   B actors   C cameramen

3 It was a great show and I got sore hands from .... so much!

   A booing   B clapping   C cheering

4 Mozart was an extraordinary .... and people still love listening to the music he wrote more than 200 years after his death.

   A composer   B conductor   C choreographer

5 This weekend I'm going to see the exhibition of dinosaur fossils that's opening at the ....

   A theatre   B art gallery   C museum

6 On Friday evening I was planning to .... but in the end I was so tired I stayed at home.

   A go out   B play up   C drop off

Task information: *Matching tasks*

You may have to match information in a box with words that you hear.
Look at this example about entertainment events.

A enjoyable for children
B no cost is involved
C requires fine weather

1 If a speaker said the following, would it match option *A*, *B* or *C*?

'… and this event will be really popular with those aged under 10.'

2 You will hear five speakers making comments about a variety of entertainment events. Listen and match what each speaker says to one of the options (A, B or C) in the box.

Speaker 1: ....

Speaker 2: ....

Speaker 3: ....

Speaker 4: ....

Speaker 5: ....

Action plan reminder for *3-option multiple-choice*

1 What should you do before you listen?
2 How do you know the answer to the next question is coming?
3 Will the words in the options (A, B and C) be the same as the words in the recording?
4 What should you do when you hear an answer?

 TIP The main speaker may be introduced by another speaker.

 TIP The questions follow the order of information in the recording.

 Questions 11–15.

*Choose the correct letter, **A**, **B** or **C**.*

11 What is new about the Writers' Festival this year?
   A more international guests
   B extra time for questions
   C additional locations for events

12 Tickets for the Wearable Art event
   A are selling out quickly.
   B have been reduced in price.
   C must be booked in advance.

13 Ocean Times at Bright's Beach is
   A a sporting competition for adults.
   B an educational event for all ages.
   C a play day for young children.

14 People going to the Artscape Exhibition
   A should wear appropriate clothing.
   B must keep to the proper path.
   C need to arrive at a certain time.

15 Tours of the Civil Theatre
   A do not happen often.
   B have never happened before.
   C may happen more regularly in future.

Advice

11 *Listen for what is new about this year's festival and watch out for distractors.*

13 *Listen for the type of event and the type of person it will appeal to.*

14 *Listen for the advice the speaker gives.*

15 *Watch out for distractors!*

TIP You may hear information in the recording that relates to all three options (**A**, **B** and **C**) but some of this is distraction.

TIP The information in the options (**A**, **B** and **C**) does not necessarily follow the order of information in the recording.

Action plan for *Matching tasks*

1   Read the instructions carefully. In some *matching tasks* you use each letter in the box more than once. In other *matching tasks* there are more options in the box and you use each letter once only.

2   Read the options in the box. Think about words you might hear that have a similar meaning.

3   Look at the names of the people, places, events, etc. that you need to match to the options.

4   Match the people, etc. with the information in the box.

5   Check your answers and then transfer them to the answer sheet at the end of the recording. Make sure you transfer the answers for both tasks!

TIP At the end of the first task there is a pause in the recording. Use this time to read the questions for the next task.

Questions 16–20

What comment does the speaker make about each of the following events?

*Write the correct letter, **A**, **B** or **C**, next to questions 16–20.*

You may use any letter more than once.

Comments

A   the location has changed

B   transport will be a problem

C   the event might be crowded

Advice

16 *Watch out for words or phrases that can have different meanings.*

17 *Listen for the words that the speaker stresses.*

18 *What advice does the speaker give?*

Events

16	Night Market	....
17	Buskers Festival	....
18	Stand Up for Kids	....
19	Sunday Unplugged	....
20	Ignite Dance Finals	....

TIP The words in the options (**A**, **B** and **C**) will not be the same as the words in the recording. Listen for synonyms and paraphrase.

Review

1. How many speakers are there?
2. What is the subject of the discussion?
3. How many tasks are there?
4. What does Part 3 test?

Now follow the Action plan reminder on pages 71-2

Useful strategy: identifying opinions

You may need to identify the opinions of speakers, rather than facts about a topic.

1. Look at the pairs of sentences below. For each pair, identify which sentence is a fact and which is an opinion.

   1. a The research sample was too small.
      b Twenty-five research subjects took part in the experiment.

   2. a It's been estimated that about 72% of Australian adults do not speak a second language.
      b More Australian adults should learn to speak a language other than English.

   3. a I didn't start learning a second language until I was an adult, when I did a course at night school for three hours a week.
      b More research should be conducted into the experiences of people who start learning a second language as adults.

   4. a Learners of English as a second language need a vocabulary of approximately 4,000 to 10,000 words.
      b The fourth edition of the *Cambridge Advanced Learner's Dictionary* contains over 140,000 words, phrases, meanings and examples, plus hundreds of pictures and illustrations.

   5. a Linguist Dr Margot McCloud claims that an adult can achieve basic fluency in a second language in three months, based on 10 hours of work per day.
      b Trying to estimate how long it will take an adult to learn a second language is a mistake because there are so many variables involved.

Useful strategy: identifying the speaker's attitude

15

1. Listen to the following excerpts. In each case, decide which option, A or B, best describes the speaker's attitude.

   1. A amused by the behaviour of other class members
      B disappointed by the actions of other class members

   2. A impressed he received the test results so quickly
      B shocked when he received his test results

   3. A surprised that vocabulary was considered so important
      B confused about why vocabulary wasn't considered more important

Action plan reminder for *5-option multiple-choice*

1 How do you know what type of information you are listening for?
2 Are the words used in the questions the same as the words in the conversation?
3 Are the two answers (options **A–E**) in the same order in the conversation?

TIP Don't use your own knowledge of a subject. Listen to what the students say.

TIP Sometimes you are listening for the speakers' opinions, not facts about the topic.

Questions 21–22

16 *Choose **TWO** letters, **A–E**.*

What **TWO** problems do the students identify with 'learning videos'?
  A Babies lose interest too quickly.
  B Babies need to explore things.
  C Babies want to be with other babies.
  D Babies' eyes may be damaged.
  E Babies should have contact with adults.

Advice

21 and **22** *Focus on problems identified by both students.*

23 and **24** *Focus on Maia's attitude towards the research.*

Questions 23–24

*Choose **TWO** letters, **A–E**.*

When discussing the 'present research', Maia is surprised that
  A ordinary people have altered their habits.
  B the findings are very detailed.
  C most babies behave the same way.
  D boys and girls like different toys.
  E the methodology has been criticised.

TIP Remember to write **TWO** letters on the answer sheet.

Questions 25–26

*Choose **TWO** letters, **A–E**.*

What impresses the students about the bilingual experiment in Spain?
  A the long-term effects of the lessons
  B the large number of research subjects
  C the fact that the children enjoyed themselves
  D the fact that teachers had the same training
  E the response of schools to the findings

Action plan reminder for *Matching tasks*

1   Can you write each letter in the box more than once?
2   Are you given time to read the questions?
3   Are the words in the box the same as the words in the recording?
4   Are the words in the questions (e.g. 27–30) the same as the recording?

TIP The questions (**27–30**) follow the order of information in the recording.

TIP The options (**A–F**) are in random order.

Questions 27–30

What was the finding of each of the following research studies?

Choose **FOUR** answers from the box and write the correct letter (**A–F**) next to **Questions 27–30**.

Findings

A Babies understand cause and effect.

B Babies like physical exercise.

C Babies like their actions to be copied.

D Babies are excited by surprises.

E Babies recognise basic grammar.

F Babies like to help other people.

Research studies

27	Dr Pritchard's study	....
28	The three-year-olds study	....
29	Professor Michelson's study	....
30	The United States study	....

Advice

27 *Listen to the end of Maia's turn before selecting the answer.*

28 *Maia asks a question. Listen carefully to Daniel's reply.*

29 *Pay particular attention to the use of paraphrase.*

TIP The speakers may suggest different possibilities or change their minds during the discussion. Listen for their final decision about an issue.

TIP There may be two or three options that you do not need to use.

Review

1. How many speakers will you hear?
2. What kind of topic might you hear?
3. How many questions do you have to answer?
4. How many tasks are there?

Now follow the Action plan reminder on page 74

Useful strategy: following the speaker

When completing notes (or a table, flow-chart, form, etc.) it is important to listen for signposting language that shows you how the text is organised. This helps you follow the speaker and locate each answer.

Here are three common types of signposting language:

    A Moving to the next stage of a lecture   B Giving an example

    C Substitution words referring to something already mentioned

1. Read these expressions and mark each one A, B or C to show what kind of signposting language it could be. For some expressions, you can use more than one letter.

1 Then, there's also the issue of …	6 The first one concerns …	11 One that stood out for me was …
2 It didn't happen then because …	7 This can be exemplified by the fact that …	12 Another aspect worth noting is …
3 By way of illustration …	8 She had some difficulties there, however, because …	13 The research attracted some criticisms as well, including …
4 The reason for this was …	9 He achieved some notable successes, such as …	14 That experiment was a success …
5 In terms of the results, the researchers found that …	10 The next thing I want to consider is …	15 Now I'd like to discuss some reasons why …

Useful strategy: editing your work

1. Look at the notes below. This candidate has essentially understood the lecture and located the correct information to fill each space. However, the candidate has made some errors recording the answers. Find the errors and correct them. Not all the notes are incorrect.

Complete the notes below.

*Write **ONE WORD ONLY** for each answer.*

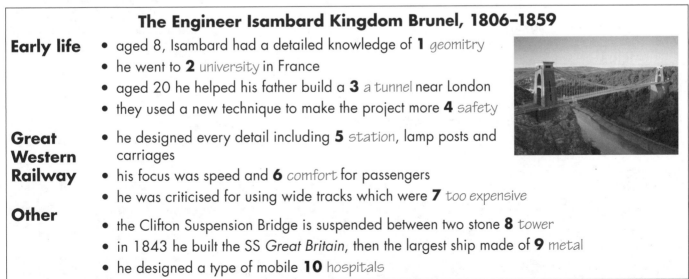

The Engineer Isambard Kingdom Brunel, 1806–1859

Early life
- aged 8, Isambard had a detailed knowledge of **1** *geomitry*
- he went to **2** *university* in France
- aged 20 he helped his father build a **3** *a tunnel* near London
- they used a new technique to make the project more **4** *safety*

Great Western Railway
- he designed every detail including **5** *station*, lamp posts and carriages
- his focus was speed and **6** *comfort* for passengers
- he was criticised for using wide tracks which were **7** *too expensive*

Other
- the Clifton Suspension Bridge is suspended between two stone **8** *tower*
- in 1843 he built the SS *Great Britain*, then the largest ship made of **9** *metal*
- he designed a type of mobile **10** *hospitals*

Action plan reminder for *Note completion*

1 How do you know how many words to write?

2 How do you know what the lecture will be about?

3 What is the best way to follow the recording?

4 How do you know what information to listen for?

Questions 31–40

17

Complete the notes.

*Write **ONE WORD ONLY** for each answer.*

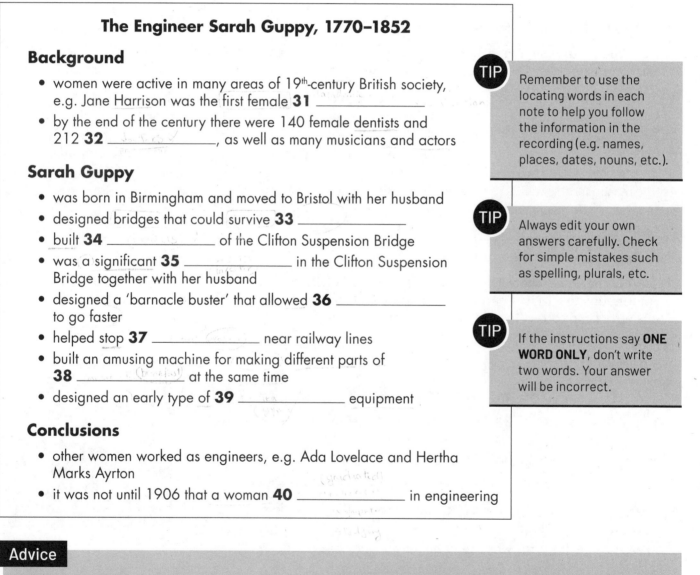

The Engineer Sarah Guppy, 1770–1852

Background

- women were active in many areas of 19th-century British society, e.g. Jane Harrison was the first female **31** _____
- by the end of the century there were 140 female dentists and 212 **32** _____, as well as many musicians and actors

Sarah Guppy

- was born in Birmingham and moved to Bristol with her husband
- designed bridges that could survive **33** _____
- built **34** _____ of the Clifton Suspension Bridge
- was a significant **35** _____ in the Clifton Suspension Bridge together with her husband
- designed a 'barnacle buster' that allowed **36** _____ to go faster
- helped stop **37** _____ near railway lines
- built an amusing machine for making different parts of **38** _____ at the same time
- designed an early type of **39** _____ equipment

Conclusions

- other women worked as engineers, e.g. Ada Lovelace and Hertha Marks Ayrton
- it was not until 1906 that a woman **40** _____ in engineering

TIP Remember to use the locating words in each note to help you follow the information in the recording (e.g. names, places, dates, nouns, etc.).

TIP Always edit your own answers carefully. Check for simple mistakes such as spelling, plurals, etc.

TIP If the instructions say **ONE WORD ONLY**, don't write two words. Your answer will be incorrect.

Advice

31 *What might her professional role have been?*

32 *The jobs listed in the question are in a different order in the recording.*

33 *Listen for something that could cause a bridge to fall down.*

35 *This must be an activity she did jointly with her husband.*

36 *There are clear locating words here. Also, listen for a synonym for **faster**.*

37 *Listen for something negative that could damage railway lines if not stopped.*

1   **Read the two short texts below (skim them quickly). What are they both about?**
    a   Exhibitions at an art gallery
    b   Displays in the building of a private company
    c   Works of art in a public library

A Long Road Home

This thought-provoking work consists of a long stretch of paved concrete that runs through the Western wing of the gallery. Artist and author Jakob Randal invites the public to contribute to the work by writing the name of their favourite book with chalk on the concrete. Western wing, entry by donation.

B The Businessman

This sculptural piece consists of a figure in a business suit seen through a series of 'mirrors', each reflecting him as a different ethnicity. While the concept behind The Businessman is distinctly international, its creator Hannah Park is one of the region's most well-known sculptors. A generous corporate endowment from GW Koos has enabled this artwork to be shown.

2   **Look at the three descriptions of events below.**

    For which events are the following statements true? Write the event name (Long Road Home or The Businessman) next to the statement.
    a   You can see work by a local artist.
    b   You can help create the artwork.
    c   You can pay as much as you want to see this exhibition.

3   **Underline the key words in the statements above and then look for them in the texts. Underline the parts of the text where you find the answer.**

You should spend about 20 minutes on **Questions 1–14**, which are based on the two texts below.

Read the text below and answer **Questions 1–7**.

TIP Read the title and headings to get an idea what the text is about.

What's on at the National Gallery of Canada?

A Governor General's Awards in Visual and Media Arts

Since 2000, the Governor General's Awards in Visual and Media Arts have acknowledged Canadian artists in the fields of fine or applied arts, film, video, or new media. This year's exhibition will showcase the work of eight outstanding laureates. Before the awards, come and greet the eight Canadian artists recognised for their remarkable contributions.

B Laurent Amiot: Canadian Master Silversmith

Acclaimed as one of the most influential silversmiths of the 18th and 19th centuries, Canadian Laurent Amiot is said to have redefined his craft, turning it into an art form.

Explore the exquisite beauty of his work through the display of nearly a hundred pivotal pieces, most of which have never been shown before.

C Artissimo Spring Forest

Come explore art – then design, draw and paint your own! Families are invited to experience the gallery and share their art with others around the world. Kids must be accompanied by an adult.

D The Ottawa Wind Ensemble presents The Music of Broadway

Enjoy an afternoon of Broadway Music in the Great Hall. The Ottawa Wind Ensemble is joined by tenor soloist Dr Fraser Rubens in a concert featuring music from famous musicals, such as *Phantom of the Opera* and *Les Misérables*. Dr Rubens' parallel careers of music and cardiac surgery have been the subject of the documentary series *The Surgeons*.

E BC Artists: from The Gary Sim collection

This exhibition allowed our curator to showcase a significant donation by collector Gary Sim, comprising almost 1,000 publications, including an extensive array of books, periodicals and other publications related to the art of western Canada. Immerse yourself in culture!

F Janet Cardiff: Forty-Part Motet

The widely acclaimed Forty-Part Motet has returned to the gallery by popular demand. The fascinating sound sculpture by artist Janet Cardiff is based on Spem in Alium, by 16th-century English composer Thomas Tallis. Voices of singers young and old are played back through forty speakers located around the Rideau Chapel in the Canadian and Indigenous galleries.

Action plan for *Locating information*

1   Will the questions be in the same order as the information is presented?
2   Will there be more than one correct answer for each question?
3   Will all mini-texts contain answers?
4   Look at the text. What will you do first?
5   Look at the questions. What will you do before you look for answers?

 TIP Use the words in the statements to find similar ideas in the text. Then read those parts of the text in more detail to see if it has the same meaning exactly.

Advice

1 **back on display** *suggests the work was in the gallery before – which artist's work does this refer to?*

2 *The question looks for something that has been* **gifted***; what word(s) in the text indicate a gift?*

3 *Look through carefully for something that means* **for the first time***. Then make sure it refers to works being exhibited.*

4 *There are several artists mentioned, but can you find someone with two careers?*

5 *Young people and kids are mentioned in two sections – which one is with reference to them coming to the event?*

6 *Artists and creative people are mentioned in several places – which one says you can meet them in person?*

7 *Which one mentions making art? Can you see any words that mean* **creating art***?*

Questions 1–7

*Look at the six descriptions of events **A–F** on page 76.*

For which events are the following statements true?

*Write the correct letter, **A–F**, in boxes 1–7 on your answer sheet.*

NB *You may use any letter more than once.*

1   You can experience a work that has been put back on display. *F*
2   You will see exhibits that have been gifted to the gallery. *E*
3   You will see works exhibited for the first time. *B*
4   You can watch a performer who is well-known in two fields. *D*
5   You can bring children to this event. *C*
6   You can meet creative people. *A*
7   You can create an artwork yourself. *C*

StarRail app and Smartcard

Use the StarRail app to get real-time updates on your journey and purchase tickets on your phone – in just a few taps, as well as the option to get alerts by email and text.

Useful features:

- View all ticket purchases through MyStarRail.
- See the status of the StarRail network and details of any disruptions to your service.
- Save recent searches to favourites.
- Contact us to report crime on the railway network.

Using a Smartcard

You can order a Smartcard using the StarRail app or get one at any StarRail station. A Smartcard is a plastic card that you can load your tickets onto.

Purchasing a ticket to put on your Smartcard: information for new users

Step 1 – purchase

Purchase tickets online using the StarRail app.

You can also get a ticket from any StarRail ticket vending machine.

Step 2 – load your Smartcard

Purchased online or with the StarRail app? Tap your Smartcard at the ticket gates or platform validator. Leave for four hours between buying and loading, so we have time to check your order and have it waiting.

Purchased at a ticket vending machine? Tap your Smartcard on the reader to load your ticket instantly.

Step 3 – tap to travel

Tap your Smartcard at the ticket gates or platform validator. Wait for the beep, then you're done. At the end of your journey, do the same again.

It costs nothing to use the app, but credit card fees may apply when buying tickets online.

Why can't I get all StarRail tickets on the app?

Our mobile booking site is under development.

You can currently purchase Advance single, Anytime and Off-Peak single and return tickets from the StarRail app. Click 'Plan & Purchase' to order these tickets.

We'll be introducing more ticket types to the StarRail app in future but for now, go to our website if you are looking for a ticket that our App does not currently offer. You can purchase all StarRail tickets (including Advance, Anytime, Off-Peak, Super Off-Peak, Kids Ride Free, Flexitix and Season Tickets) using our desktop booking website.

Smartcard benefits:
Season tickets

You can load weekly, monthly and annual Season Tickets for all our routes.

Super off-peak day return

These tickets are exclusive to Smartcard: enjoy great savings when you travel outside peak hours from Monday to Friday.

Action plan reminder for *True / False / Not given*

1 Are the questions in the same order as the information you need to find in text?

2 Will there always be at least one **True**, one **False** and one **Not Given** answer?

3 Will all paragraphs contain answers?

4 Look at the text, what will you do first?

5 Look at the questions. What will you do before you look for answers?

TIP Use the words in the statements to find the part of the text you need to read carefully for each question. Remember – the text may use different words from the questions.

Advice

8 *Find the part of the text that mentions problems on the train line but uses different words.*

9 *Find the information about vending machines (Step 1). Does the text say how you must pay at a vending machine?*

10 *Look for the information that refers to buying and loading tickets with the app. Now read the paragraph carefully and answer the question.*

11 *Find the part of the text about ticket validators (Step 3). Does the text tell you whether there are validators on all platforms?*

12 *Look for words, such as price / cost / fee, etc. – make sure the words refer to the cost of the app.*

13 *Find the part that mentions Flexitix. Some tickets can be purchased via the app, while others are only available on the desktop website. Which category is Flexitix in?*

14 *Find words that refer to **quiet times**. Read that part of the text carefully and answer the question. If you found the information for the previous question about Flexitix, remember that question 14 will be after that in the text.*

TIP If you find the right place in the text but you can't find the answer, you should write 'Not given'.

Questions 8–14

Do the following statements agree with the information given in Reading Passage 1?

In boxes 8–14 on your answer sheet, write

TRUE	*if the statement agrees with the information*
FALSE	*if the statement contradicts the information*
NOT GIVEN	*if there is no information on this*

8 The app lets passengers know if there are problems on the train line.

9 Tickets purchased from vending machines must be paid for by credit card centre.

10 Tickets bought on the internet are loaded onto Smartcard immediately.

11 All stations have ticket validators on platforms.

12 The SmartRail app is free of charge.

13 Passengers can buy Flexitix using the app.

14 Cheaper tickets are available for those travelling at quiet times.

1   **Read the text below. What is it about?**
    a   Instructions about how to operate a forklift safely
    b   A session about what forklift drivers in one company need to know
    c   Advice about how to get a job as a forklift driver in a factory

Larrington Plastics

Training Schedule for forklift drivers

Your first day will begin at 9 a.m. when our foreman Greg Shaw will give an outline of what the job of forklift driver entails. This will take place in our warehouse behind the car park. After this, we will run through how we keep track of inventory. We use RF scanners for inventory management, and this is an opportunity to practise using these if you're unfamiliar with them and to ask questions. Finally, you'll be shown where the forklifts are kept, and we'll cover some essential points in relation to their maintenance. You will then meet the rest of your co-workers at the canteen for morning tea.

2   **Complete the flow-chart below.**
    Choose **ONE WORD ONLY** from the text for each answer.

3   **Find the parts of the text that give the information to fill each space and underline the words you need.**
    Which words in the text let you know that the writer has moved on to a new step?

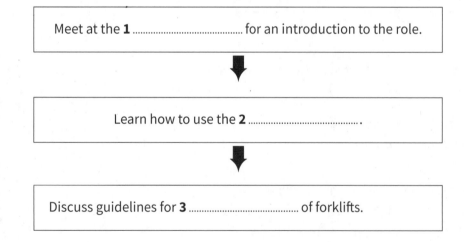

Meet at the **1** .... for an introduction to the role.

⬇

Learn how to use the **2** ....

⬇

Discuss guidelines for **3** .... of forklifts.

*You should spend about 20 minutes on **Questions 15–27**, which are based on Reading Passage 2 below.*

*Read the text below and answer **Questions 15–21**.*

Fruit Picking Work in Australia

Because Australia is such a large place, it has several weather zones and many different crops are grown. This means that there is usually work for fruit pickers somewhere in the country. It's worth remembering that there are other related jobs available after the harvest period, such as pruning and planting.

If you're interested in picking fruit in Australia, plan well and be prepared to work hard!

Here are some tips to help you:

Working in the sun

- Wearing sunglasses, to avoid the glare, and sunscreen is absolutely essential if you want to avoid sunburn. A long-sleeved cotton shirt may not seem appealing, but you will be thankful for it in the heat of the day.
- Keeping hydrated is crucial. You will find that you may drink up to eight litres of water a day if you are working outside. It will save time if you keep your water in something that is clipped onto your belt so that you can take a drink whenever you need to.

Other requirements

- Every farm is different. Sometimes, employers don't supply tools, so workers need to use their own. Check first to make sure you have what you need.
- Consider taking an MP3 player or another device so that you can listen to music. The days can be long, and it makes the time go faster.

Various roles

- Instead of working in the orchard, you may find yourself in a packing shed. There is a lot to be done here too, from packing fruit into boxes, checking quality control and using a forklift to loading large pallets onto trucks.

Payment methods

- Fruit should not be picked when wet so, in the case of rain, you will have to stop work. Therefore, you will not be paid in most instances.
- Some farms pay a flat rate (by the hour), but getting a fixed amount is not common for work that involves collecting fruit; this type of payment is generally for work in the shed. The other, more usual, model is the piece rate: your pay depends on the amount of fruit you bring in at the end of the day.

Remember conditions vary greatly from farm to farm so be sure to check anything you need to know with the employer before you start.

Action plan for *Sentence completion*

1 What do the title and headings tell you about the text?

2 Are the questions in the same order as the information you need to find in text?

3 Look at the text. What will you do first?

4 Look at the questions. What will you do before you look for answers?

5 What is the maximum number of words that you can write in each space?

 TIP Mark the words you need in the text. Then double-check that they fit in terms of grammar and meaning.

Advice

15 *Look at the space. In this case, you need a word that can come before* **time** *and is a noun.*

16 *Two things are mentioned along with clothing – what is something that protects the body?*

17 *Find the part of the text that refers to drinking water. What should the bottle be attached to?*

18 *Look under the heading* **Other requirements**. *The text refers to two things you might bring. Which of these might you have to bring?*

19 *Look under the heading* **Various roles**. *What is a forklift used for?*

20 *The question mentions money. Which heading should you look under in the text?*

21 *You need two words here. What is the term for pay related to picking fruit?*

Questions 15–21

Complete the sentences below.

Choose **NO MORE THAN TWO WORDS** *from the text for each answer.*

Write your answers in boxes 15–21 on your answer sheet.

Fruit Picking in Australia

Sometimes there are employment opportunities following the **15** .... time when fruit is picked.

Wearing appropriate clothing, eyewear and **16** .... is necessary to protect your body.

It is recommended to take a water bottle that can be attached to a **17** ....

It is necessary for fruit pickers to bring **18** .... if these are not provided.

Other jobs on the farm may involve moving big **19** ....

20 .... can affect how much work is done and how much money is earned.

Most picking jobs pay workers a **21** ....

Haast legal services: Orientation day for new employees

HAAST LEGAL SERVICES

Here at Haast, we run regular staff-orientation sessions for our new employees. In your first week with Haast, you can expect to attend an orientation program to help you familiarise yourself with the workplace. Generally, this will be conducted for groups of three or more. Below is a rough outline for the day:

9:00 Induction session, Boardroom 2

Here you will learn about the history of our company and meet some of our team. Our HR manager will take you through what is expected of employees from an HR policy perspective and outline the chief priorities of our firm.

10:15 Tour, morning tea, Cafeteria

Our office manager will take you around the office to show you where everything is, including bathroom facilities, stationery and photocopying, first aid kit and payroll. You'll finish in the cafeteria where you'll have the chance to speak to our administrative support staff as well as some of the executives who sit on the board. This is an informal yet important part of the day.

11:00 Sensitive information awareness, Boardroom 3

Here at Haast we often deal with matters of a sensitive nature whether they be personal / family disputes or financial difficulties. This requires a clear understanding of privacy concerns and a commitment to respecting our clients' information. One of our senior staff will outline our policies.

12:30 Lunch

1:30 HR session, 1 Atrium

Be here after lunch to have your photo taken. You will be issued with an employee card (which can be collected from reception at the end of the day). Topics that will be covered include how to apply for various types of leave, submission of timesheets and our dress code.

2:30 Training in your own department

This is where you will learn more about your specific position. If possible, you will join the person who previously held your role for a handover. If this is not possible, your team leader will tell you what you need to know.

Online modules

You will have a week to complete two online modules which cover Haast's sustainability policy and safety in the workplace. Feedback will be given via the portal or in person if necessary.

Action plan for *Flow-chart completion*

1. Look at the title and any headings and decide what the text is about.
2. Read the text very quickly to get a general idea of its structure and ideas.
3. Read the flow-chart quickly and see how many words you must write for each space.
4. Read the flow-chart carefully and underline important words.
5. Find the part of the text which contains the same information as the flow-chart.
6. Read the relevant part of the text carefully and underline the word that you think fits in the space.
7. Transfer the information to the answer sheet.

 TIP You will not need to change the word you copy, e.g. from a noun to an adjective or from singular to plural.

TIP Some parts of the flow-chart may not have a space in them. These help you find the right part of the text.

Questions 22–27

Complete the flow-chart below.

*Choose **ONE WORD AND / OR A NUMBER** from the text for each answer.*

Write your answers in boxes 22–27 on your answer sheet.

Haast New Recruits: Orientation Day

General induction session:
- background of organisation
- expectations at work (HR)
- the organisation's main **22** ....

Meet in Reception, session in Boardroom 2

▼

Tour, Morning tea:
- meet members of the **23** .... and the admin team

Cafeteria

▼

Information awareness session:
- introduction to issues relating to **24** ....

Boardroom 3

▼

Lunch

▼

HR:
- go to **25** .... for employee photo

Training:
- start **26** .... with predecessor or manager in particular roles

Various departments

▼

- finish training about environmental impact and **27** .... matters within the week

Online

Advice

22 Look under the **Induction session** heading in the text. The background and expectations of the organisation are mentioned in the flow-chart. What else will be covered in that session?

23 Find the part of the text about morning tea. Who will be there?

24 Look at the **Sensitive information awareness session**. What issue might some sensitive information raise?

25 Look at the flow-chart and predict what kind of information you will need. A room and reception are mentioned in this paragraph – which one is correct? Remember you can write a word and a number if you need to.

26 Look at what happens after the HR session.

27 What is done online?

1 Read the text below (skim it quickly for the main idea). What is it about?
   a Frida Kahlo's personal life
   b Frida Kahlo's travels
   c Frida Kahlo's art

In the 1940s, Frida Kahlo produced many paintings though with some differences from what she had done before. She was encouraged by the public recognition she was gaining and shifted from using the small tin sheets she had used since 1932 to much larger canvases, as they were easier to exhibit. She also adopted a more sophisticated technique and began to produce larger, quarter-length portraits than she had previously, which were easier to sell. Kahlo created many of her most famous pieces during this period, for instance *Self-Portrait with Cropped Hair* (1940), *The Wounded Table* (1940), and *Self-Portrait with Thorn Necklace and Hummingbird* (1940).

2 Choose the correct letter, **a, b, c** or **d**.
   Why did Kahlo start making her paintings a different size?
   a She had more room in her studio for larger artworks.
   b She was unable to find large pieces of tin to paint on.
   c Smaller works were more convenient to hang in galleries.
   d People wanted to buy paintings of a certain size.

3 Read the stem (the question) of the multiple-choice without reading all the options and think about what the answer might be. Then read the options and consider how they are different from each other. Finally, look at the text and underline where you think the answer is.

You should spend about 20 minutes on **Questions 28–40**, which are based on the text below.

Read the text below and answer **Questions 28–40**.

Freya Stark

Freya Stark was a British explorer and writer who had several works published about her travels in the Middle East and Afghanistan, as well as autobiographies and essays.

Born in Paris in 1893, Freya Stark was raised in Italy and England. As a child, she spoke several languages and her upbringing included many outdoor pursuits, like horse riding and mountaineering. With her mother and grandmother as role models, she developed into an unconventional woman who was as at home in elegant salons as she was able to handle hardship and physical exertion.

In 1912, Stark started studying history in London but left for Bologna, Italy, at the beginning of the First World War, to work as a nurse. In 1918, her father gave her a small estate in Mortola on the Riviera in northern Italy, where she grew grapes, vegetables and flowers. But she often travelled to England to take Arabic language courses at the School of Oriental and African Studies. She was nearly thirty by this time. A professor had suggested that she try a non-European language: he recommended Icelandic. Stark, who had been struggling to make a living on the farm in Italy, chose Arabic in the hope that it might provide an opportunity to get away. She had developed a desire to travel to the Middle East and, to this end, applied for the role of governess for the Iraqi princesses at the court of Baghdad, Iraq, but was not successful.

In 1927, she travelled to Lebanon and then on to Damascus, Syria. Travel in the area was restricted at the time, so Stark set off from Damascus in secret on a donkey with a local guide and an English female friend, who had come to join the trip. Stark took pride in travelling without servants or extra belongings, comparing herself favourably in this regard to writer and explorer Gertrude Bell, an Oxford-educated aristocrat who had completed a similar trip with three baggage mules, two tents and three servants. Stark considered herself a more intrepid traveller.

After this, Stark returned to London and went to the Royal Geographical Society to take drawing courses so that she would be able to make her own maps on future trips. In 1929, she set off again for the Middle East and in 1930, Stark reached Persia (now known as Iran). She visited the Valleys of the Assassins, at the time still unexplored by Europeans, and carried out geographical and archaeological studies. On the back of a mule, with a camp bed and a mosquito net, and accompanied by a local guide, Freya Stark rode to the valleys near Alamut to see ruins of a mountain fortress castle which had not yet been recorded on her map. Despite malaria, dengue fever and dysentery, she carried on with her trip and her studies.

Stark's books present a combination of adventure and harsh reality. In *The Southern Gates of Arabia* she tells of following the ancient trade route for the perfumed substance frankincense in the area that is present-day Yemen. Unfortunately, she had to turn back without realising the goal she had set of finding the legendary lost city of Shabwa.

In 1944, Stark spent time in New Delhi, India at the court of the British viceroy. During political discussions there she met renowned politicians, Gandhi and Nehru. She was a regular guest at parties and official functions, where she became known for her extravagant clothes as well as her life of adventure.

While she did not make any huge new discoveries as an explorer, Freya Stark gained a high degree of respect for her sharp observations and compelling tales of her travels. She was able to accurately record unmarked villages and mountains, using compass points and photographs, but people read her books for the descriptions of the journey.

Often Stark would be the only European woman to have visited the places she travelled to, and often she discovered that the only people available to speak with her were the women. Stark might have approached women as a way of gaining trust and reaching powerful men, but over time she got specialised knowledge of the domestic arrangements, costumes and children's lives in these places thanks to her contact with women.

Stark was not especially interested in politics, beyond a desire to remedy the injustices she saw first-hand on her travels. Her main interest was archaeology. However, her later books such as *Rome on the Euphrates*, which came out in 1966, was criticised at the time for being overloaded with history and less in the genre of travel book, which is what readers seemed to want from her. Her last significant trip was to Afghanistan, in 1968, when she was 75. She went to see a 12th-century minaret that had only shortly beforehand been discovered by archaeologists.

Stark kept writing throughout her 80s and early 90s (four volumes of autobiography and eight volumes of letters), the last of which was published in 1985 when she was 93. She travelled until she was 92 and lived to be 100 years of age. Towards her final years, she took many of her godchildren on trips to inspire and educate them, telling them what she had learned from those she met along the way. Freya Stark produced 22 books in her lifetime and serves as an inspiration to travel writers to this day.

Action plan for *Matching places*

If the *matching places* questions are the first task for a text, read the text quickly first to get an idea of the general structure and information in the text.

1   Look at the list of places. Find them in the text and underline them.

2   For each place, read all of the information given about it in the text.

3   For each place, choose the statement which matches one of the things that happened at that place.

 TIP Sometimes the place names are in more than one part of the text.

Advice

28 What is another word for **social event**? In which place did Stark go to such events?

29 Where can you find examples of poor health?

30 Look at each place. Does it say anything about employment / a job?

31 What was it that would help Stark on her travels? Look at each place for a reference of learning to do something she would later find useful when she travelled.

32 Can you find a phrasal verb that means **leave**? Where did Stark have to do this?

Questions 28–32

*Look at the following statements (**Questions 28–32**) and the list of places below.*

*Match each statement with the correct place, **A–F**.*

*Write the correct letter **A–F** in boxes 28–32 on your answer sheet.*

***NB** you may use any letter more than once.*

28   Stark attended many social events.

29   Stark suffered from poor health.

30   Stark failed to gain employment.

31   Stark learnt a craft that would help her on her journeys.

32   Stark had to leave without achieving her purpose.

List of Places

A   Baghdad
B   London
C   Alamut
D   Yemen
E   New Delhi
F   Afghanistan

Action plan for *Multiple-choice*

1   How many correct options can you choose for each question?
2   Are the questions in the same order as the information in the text?
3   Should you read and answer each question in turn?
4   How much of the text should you read for each question?
5   Should you answer the questions using your general knowledge?
6   Look at the text. What will you do first?
7   Look at the questions. What will you do before you look for answers?

 TIP Read the text quickly. Then read it more carefully as you answer each question in turn.

Advice

33 *Which word in the question tells you where to look for the answer in the text? (Arabic)*

34 *Look for information on Gertrude Bell. The options mention time, baggage, education and the route – all concepts that are in the text – but in which respect does Stark compare herself to Bell?*

35 *Look at the paragraph fourth from the end. The concepts in the options are all mentioned in some way but which concept in the text is accurately reflected in one of the options?*

36 *Can you find the paragraph where Stark's interaction with women is discussed? Remember it should be somewhere after the part of the text on which the previous question was based.*

Questions 33–36

*Choose the correct letter **A, B, C** or **D**.*

Write the correct letter in boxes 33–36 on your answer sheet.

33 What influenced Stark's decision to learn Arabic?
   A   An academic advised her to choose that particular language.
   B   She planned to accompany a friend to the Middle East.
   C   She wanted to escape her situation at the time.
   D   The language had always held an interest for her.

34 How did Stark compare herself to Gertrude Bell?
   A   She made the journey from Damascus to Syria in less time than Bell did.
   B   She took less baggage on her trip than Bell took.
   C   She had a better education than Bell had.
   D   She took a more exciting route from Damascus than Bell took.

35 What does the writer say about Freya Stark as an explorer?
   A   She was the first to find some major landmarks.
   B   She deserved more recognition than she received.
   C   She produced interesting accounts of her expeditions.
   D   She drew some unreliable maps.

36 According to the writer, why did Stark become an expert on the lives of women in the places she went to?
   A   She gained access to women more easily than to men.
   B   She was more interested in the lives of women than of men.
   C   She met them while studying their traditional costumes.
   D   She was introduced to local women by other female travellers.

Action plan for *Summary completion*

1   What does the summary heading tell you about where to look in the text?
2   What kinds of words will you need to put in the space
    (e.g. noun, verb, adjective)?
3   Look at the text, what will you do first?
4   Look at the questions. What will you do before you look for answers?
5   What is the maximum number of words that you can write in each space?

TIP Key words such as place names and names of books in the summary can help you find where to look in the text.

Advice

37 *Look for the name of the book 'Rome on the Euphrates'. What did people say about the book at the time?*

38 *Find information about Stark's trip to Afghanistan late in her life? What was her reason for going there?*

39 *What did Stark publish besides books?*

40 *Who did Stark take on trips when she was older?*

Questions 37–40

Complete the summary below.

*Choose **ONE WORD ONLY** from the text for each answer.*

Write your answers in boxes 37–40 on your answer sheet.

Freya Stark's later years

Stark's book *Rome on the Euphrates* was said to focus too heavily on **37** .... rather than what her audience had come to expect. Stark's motivation for going to Afghanistan when she was 75 was to visit an ancient **38** .... In her old age, she continued to publish collections of **39** .... along with books about her life. She was often accompanied by her **40** .... when she travelled.

Review

1 How long should you spend on this task?

2 How many words do you have to write?

3 Do you have to write about each of the points?

4 Should you make up extra points to write about?

5 What type of writing will you always have to do for Writing Task 1?

6 Do you have to use a formal style every time?

7 Are vocabulary and spelling tested?

8 Are grammar and punctuation tested?

Now follow the Action plan reminder on page 95

Useful language: giving advice and suggestions

1 **Read the sentences (1–5) carefully. Then answer questions a and b for each sentence.**

   a How well does the writer know the reader?

   b Is the tone formal, neutral or informal?

   1 Perhaps you could think about living near me in Bondi.

   2 It is recommended that employees reside near their workplace.

   3 We suggest that you should live near the office.

   4 Why don't you just move in down the road from my mum?

   5 You ought to consider Bondi as a place to live.

2 **Underline any useful words or phrases (above) that you might use when giving advice in a letter.**

Useful language: punctuation

Punctuation helps make your meaning clear to the reader and separates ideas so that they can be understood.

1 Add punctuation marks to the text.

> Secondly while it is commonly believed that our city's public transport system is one of the most efficient in the country this is not true in peak hours for example between 8 and 9:30 a.m. when people are travelling to school and work so there is certainly more that can be done to keep traffic moving decrease wait times and ensure that everyone gets where they need to go as quickly as possible

2 Some of the statements below need to be broken into two sentences and some should be one sentence. Mark correct sentences with ✓. Add punctuation to incorrect sentences.

1 I haven't heard back from my manager about taking leave in July which is why I haven't been in touch.

2 It isn't a long way from the airport to my house however you should take a taxi if you have heavy luggage with you.

3 The sales assistant left me with no choice but to complain to the manager. Because it was clear that he didn't have the authority to give a refund.

4 Although it can be an expensive place to visit, New York is a place you will never forget.

5 I have a lot of experience in organising parties and festivals. For this reason, I believe I would be perfect for the role of event planner.

6 I am writing to request some help with the extra duties I have been given, I do not feel able to cope with my current workload and am falling behind.

Useful language: finishing a letter

1 When you finish a letter, think about the purpose of the letter you've just written and what you expect the reader to do. You also need to think about how well you know the reader.

Match the functions (1–5) with the different ways to end a letter (a–e). There may be more than one option for each.

1 Asking for information
2 Complaining
3 Giving information
4 Requesting a favour
5 Offering to help

a Many thanks.
b If I do not hear from you soon, I will have to escalate this matter.
c I look forward to hearing from you soon.
d If you have any questions, please do not hesitate to contact me.
e Let me know if there's anything else I can do.

2 If you are writing a formal letter to someone you do not know or complaining, there are specific ways to sign off.

Which of the following go together?

1 Dear Sir or Madam
2 Dear Mr Phuong
a Yours sincerely
b Yours faithfully

3 If you know the person, any of these may be appropriate ways to sign off, depending on the situation.

Put these in order from the least personal to the most personal.

| Best wishes | Bye for now | Cheers | Lots of love |
| Regards | Take care | Warm regards | |

....

....

....

....

....

....

....

Useful language: phrasal verbs

Phrasal verbs (verb + particle, e.g. *take off*) can help a letter read naturally. Some phrasal verbs are very common and are used in formal, neutral and informal situations, e.g. *The plane will* **take off** *when the weather improves.* Others are less formal, e.g. *The kids were* **hanging out** *near the station.*

1 Match the phrasal verbs (1–6) with their meanings (a–f).

1	bring up	a	investigate
2	get away with	b	analyse
3	look into	c	mention
4	break down	d	avoid punishment
5	fill in for	e	inconvenience someone
6	put someone out	f	substitute for

2 Add the phrasal verbs from the list in Exercise 1 to the following sentences. You may need to change the verb form, e.g. to the past tense.

1 We need to .... the data to see why sales have dropped.
2 I wish he hadn't .... the subject of our disastrous holiday.
3 The police are .... the theft of two cars from our street.
4 I'm hoping Fred can .... for me on the night shift.
5 I'd love a lift home, but I don't want to ....
6 If you cheat on the test, you won't .... it because security is tight.

Useful language: striking the right tone

1 What is wrong with the following expressions / sentences? Can you correct them?

Dear friend,

Dear Lisa Reynolds,

Dear Manager,

Your staff are always very friendly, but I demand a refund.

Hi Jerry – I'm writing to inform you of my intention to move to Ottawa.

Please accept my heartfelt apology for taking up your time with this letter.

I left my last job coz of my boss.

Action plan reminder

1 Look at Writing Task 1 below.
- Who should you write to?
- What three points do you need to cover?
- Can you think of a part of the city that is a good place to live?
- What words do you know to describe public transport?

2 Think about your answer for Writing Task 1.
- How should you begin the letter? Do you need to write a person's name?
- Which city are you going to write about? Should you give the name of the city?
- How can a person make a new life when they move to a different city?
- What will the tone of the letter be?
- How will you finish your letter?

Before you write

3 Make brief notes on each of the bullet points in Exercise 1 and 2.

4 Write your letter.
- If you don't live in a city, should you write about a whole country?
- Should you include points that are not in the task?
- Do you need to write an equal amount on each point?
- Should you take a formal tone?

After you write

5 What should you check for when you have finished? (see page 49)

 Remember not to take longer than 20 minutes for Writing Task 1.

 Double-check that you have written something for each bullet point.

Advice

How can you take a friendly tone in a letter to a friend?

What phrases are used for giving advice?

Writing Task 1

You should spend about 20 minutes on this task.

A friend from another country is moving to your city for work. He / she has asked you for advice about living in your city.

Write a letter to your friend. In your letter

- ***suggest an interesting part of the city to live in***
- ***describe the public transport in your city***
- ***say how your friend can meet new people there***

Write at least 150 words.

You do **NOT** need to write any addresses.

Begin your letter as follows:

Dear .... ,

Review

1 What is Writing Task 2?
2 Which of these things does it test?
   - academic knowledge
   - general knowledge
   - expressing ideas
   - having clever opinions
   - vocabulary
   - grammar
   - spelling
   - punctuation
   - organisation of ideas
   - paragraphing
3 How many words do you need to write?
4 What should you do in your introduction?
5 How should you support your opinion?
6 How should you finish your essay?

Now follow the Action plan reminder on page 97

Useful language: reporting what people say and believe

1 **Choose the correct form of the words in italics to complete the sentences.**
   1 It *is often said / often is saying* that people need a university education.
   2 Some people believe that further education *to be / is* essential.
   3 In the past, most people felt that it *was / had been* more important to have experience rather than qualifications.
   4 Workers in some areas consider university *to be / is* a waste of time.
   5 It is *widely / greatly* accepted that a good education leads to a successful career.
   6 According to *me / experts*, the first year is the most important for a new business.

2 **Use the words in brackets to complete the sentences. You may need to change the verb into the correct form.**
   1 It .... (sometimes, argue) that robots will soon be doing jobs that are currently done by humans.
   2 Technology .... (consider, be) a positive thing in most people's lives.
   3 Experts .... (be, in agreement) that too much screen time has a negative effect on people of all ages.
   4 While some .... (do, not agree with) the idea of wearing a school uniform, I believe it makes school life simpler for everyone.
   5 It .... (widely, believe) that the government should do all it can to look after its most vulnerable citizens.

Useful language: countable and uncountable nouns

1 **Choose the correct form of the words in italics to complete the sentences.**
   1 The government's top priority should be *education / an education*.
   2 My grandfather didn't have the chance to get *good education / a good education*.
   3 A large *amount / number* of people attend outdoor music festivals.
   4 The statement made by the workers *were / was* not considered by management.
   5 Playing computer games can be harmful but it depends *how much time / how many times* you spend doing it.
   6 There *isn't enough space / aren't enough spaces* for everyone to live in a small house.

Useful language: giving two sides of an argument

Here are some examples of comments that do not agree or disagree completely with one view.

1 **Match the clauses (1–4) with the clauses (a–d) to make sentences.**

1 While a university education is still required in some fields of work,
2 Whereas some students like wearing a uniform,
3 Although tourism brings economic benefits,
4 Cooking food at home can take a long time,

a it can also threaten the local way of life.
b but it does cost less than going out.
c in many other fields work experience is preferred.
d others want to express their own style.

2 **Complete the sentences below about each of the five topics in the box.**

> banning cars in the city centre   eating in restaurants   using mobile phones
> making people pay for plastic bags   working in a different country

1 While ....
2 Whereas ....
3 Although ....
4 ....
5 .... However, ...

Action plan reminder

1   Look at Writing Task 2 below.

   How long should you spend on this task?

   How many questions do you need to answer?

   To help you plan, what should you underline in the task?

   Should you copy the exact wording of the task?

Before you write

2   Make notes before you begin. What should your notes include?

After you write

3   Should you spend time checking your answer when you have finished? If so, how much time should you allow for this?

4   Should you write your essay out again if you have made mistakes?

5   Which of the following should you check for?
   - where to start and end sentences
   - overall structure
   - formal / neutral / informal style
   - subject-verb agreement
   - memorised quotations from experts
   - accurate statistics to back up your ideas
   - spelling
   - paragraphing
   - whether you have made clear points

Writing Task 2

You should spend about 40 minutes on this task.

Write about the following topic:

Many people believe that a university education is necessary for a good career.

Do you agree or disagree?

What other factors can contribute to a good career?

Give reasons for your answer and include any relevant examples from your own knowledge or experience.

Write at least 250 words.

Advice

*A word like **university** is hard to paraphrase. Can you put it in a sentence in a different way, so that it doesn't come before **education** (as it does in the task)?*

Do some careers require a university education more than others do?

How can people have a good career if they do not go to university?

 TIP When you are practising for the exam, make sure you know what 250 words looks like in your handwriting. How many words do you usually fit on each line? You do not want to waste time counting each word in the test.

TIP You don't need to completely agree or disagree with the statement. You can say in which cases you agree and in which cases you disagree.

Review Speaking Part 1

1 What kind of topic do you have to talk about in Part 1?

2 What is the first topic?

3 How many different topics will you be asked to talk about?

4 How many questions are there for each topic?

5 What must you take with you to the exam room?

Useful language: where you live

The examiner will either start the test by asking you about your work / studies or about where you live. This could be the city / town you live in or your home – your house / apartment.

1 Think about your home. What can you say about it? Look at the words in the table and add any other words to describe it.

Building	block of apartments apartment on the ground / fifth floor cottage detached / terraced house
Area	a busy / quiet area in the centre of the city in the mountains in a suburb in a village on the coast on a housing estate on the outskirts
Style of home	cosy light modern spacious traditional
Special features	lovely views of … balcony garden gym swimming pool terrace

2 How do you feel about your home? Complete these sentences.

1 I love my home because it's ....

2 My home makes me feel ....

3 My favourite room in my home is ....

4 The thing I like most about my home is ....

5 I enjoy spending time at home especially when ....

3 Look at the questions about your home on page 104 and practise answering them. Use some of the words and phrases in Exercises 1 and 2.

Useful language: tenses

The questions in Part 1 are often in the present tense, but other tenses are also used. It is important to listen carefully to the question and use the correct tense in your answer.

1 Complete the questions that go with these answers.

1 Where ....?   I live in the capital city.

2 How long ....?   We've lived in this apartment for 10 years.

3 Why ....?   My father got a new job, so we moved here.

4 ....?   Yes, I'd like to live by the sea one day.

5 ....?   No, I don't think we'll move for a long time.

2 Now answer these questions using the correct tense.

1 How long have you been studying English? ....

2 Why did you start learning English? ....

3 What other language would you like to learn? ....

4 What do you like most about learning English? ....

5 Do you think you will live in the UK in the future? ....

 TIP Remember to extend your answer by adding a reason or an example.

Useful language: the weather

1   Think about different weather conditions in your country and how they make you feel.

sunshine / sunny – happy / hot / tired

rain / rainy – ....

shower / showery – ....

thunderstorm / stormy – ....

clouds / cloudy – ....

fog / foggy – ....

snow / snowy – ....

wind / windy – ....

2   Look at the questions about the weather on page 104 and the beginnings of the sentences below.

My favourite kind of weather is when it's . . .

I hate it when it . . .

Cloudy weather really makes me feel . . .

If I'm studying hard I prefer the weather to be . . .

When I was little I loved . . .

I'd really like to live in a country where . . .

3   Now practise saying your answers. Record yourself and check your answers carefully. Did you use the right tenses? Did you give a reason or example in each answer? Did you speak clearly?

Review Speaking Part 2

1   Which three things will the examiner give you?

2   How long will you have to prepare?

3   Where should you write any notes?

4   How long should you talk for?

5   When will the examiner ask questions?

Ways to prepare for the talk

In Test 1 we looked at how to make notes in the one-minute preparation time. Making notes is a good strategy but it may not suit everyone. Some people prefer not to write anything. They look at the task and think carefully about each point. Other people like to do other things, such as making a spider diagram.

1   Here is an exam task. Look at each of the points and think about what you want to say about each one. Don't write anything.

> *Describe a time when someone gave you some very helpful advice.*
>
> > **You should say**
> > > **when this happened and where you were**
> > > **who the person was**
> > > **what advice he or she gave you**
> >
> > **and explain why the advice you received was very helpful.**

 TIP Read the task carefully and pay attention to the key words.

2   Now look at the empty spider diagram and write a few words in each bubble for each point in the task.

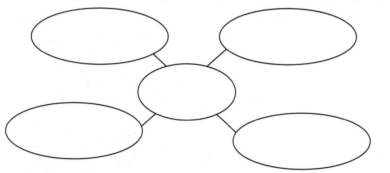

TIP It doesn't matter which order you talk about the different task points but try to give your talk a logical structure.

3   Give a two-minute talk about the advice you were given.

4   Decide which strategy suits you best – making notes, drawing a spider diagram, thinking but not writing anything, or another preparation method.

Useful strategies: problems and solutions for giving a talk

When you are giving your talk, you may not always be able to find the precise word you want. This happens to everyone and the important thing is not to panic or leave a long silence. There are two things you can do.

Use a 'filler' to give yourself time to think while you search for the word. Here are some examples.

. . . what I mean to say is . . .

. . . how can I put this . . .

. . . let me think . . .

. . . I'm not quite sure of the word, but . . .

If the word still doesn't come, then go around it by using a paraphrase. Here is a paraphrase for the word 'fog':
I really hate the kind of weather, you know when you can't see anything. It can be very dangerous.

1 **Try making paraphrases for these words.**

  1 an oven ....

  2 a scholarship ....

  3 a guarantee ....

  4 a prize ....

  5 a warning ....

2 **Look at the task about a problem on page 104. Take one minute to prepare using your favourite preparation strategy. Then record yourself giving the talk. Use a timer and make sure you speak for two minutes.**

> **TIP** If you speak for less than two minutes the examiner will ask you to continue and may suggest you say more about one of the task points.

3 **Look at the two rounding off questions after the task on page 104 and answer them.**

4 **Listen to your talk and answer these questions.**

- Was there a clear introduction?
- Were all the four task points covered?
- Was the vocabulary varied?
- Were you speaking clearly – too fast or too slowly?
- Were there any grammar mistakes, e.g. 's' missing at the end of he / she verbs?
- Was the talk long enough?
- Were there any spaces where you were searching for words?

5 **Think about the answers to the questions and what you can do to improve your talk. Then record yourself giving the talk again.**

> **TIP** Don't try to give a talk you have learnt by heart. It will not sound natural and you may talk about something which is not appropriate or relevant. This may affect your marks.

Review Speaking Part 3

1 What topic will the questions be about?

2 Will the questions focus on your personal experience?

3 How many questions will you have to answer?

Useful language: hesitation devices

In Part 2 we looked at phrases that can give you time to think when you're searching for words in the middle of your talk. Other useful phrases can help you while you are trying to think of ideas when the examiner asks you a question, especially if it is one you have never considered before. It is not good to say nothing or just 'um . . . er'.

1 **Look at the hesitation devices in the box. Practise using them when answering the questions below.**

> *Oh, that's an interesting / a difficult question.*
>
> *I've never thought about that, but I'd say . . .*
>
> *Well, on the whole I tend to think that . . .*
>
> *That really depends on the situation, of course, but . . .*
>
> *I think the key thing here is . . .*
>
> *I'm not an expert in . . ., but I suppose that . . .*

1 Do you think young people have fewer problems today than their grandparents did?

2 It's said that the world will run out of food in the next century. What do you think?

3 Will scientists always come up with answers to the problems humanity faces?

Useful language: speaking generally

You are expected to give your opinions on general issues in Part 3 and not to describe personal experiences.

1 Answer the questions. Start by using a phrase in the box below to introduce a general point and then continue by expressing your own opinion.

Example: Do people help their neighbours enough nowadays?

'In many cases people are unwilling to help their neighbours because they don't want to interfere. However, I believe that we should always offer to help our neighbours, especially the elderly. After all, they can always say "No, thank you".'

1 Will computer-based learning ever replace classroom teaching?

2 How soon will space tourism become an affordable option?

3 Do international sporting events really help people to understand other cultures or do they increase nationalism?

4 Is there any point in individuals recycling plastic when there's so much plastic waste in the oceans?

> *In many cases, . . .*
>
> *Generally speaking, . . .*
>
> *Most people accept / recognise / believe that . . .*
>
> *That depends on the circumstances, but . . .*
>
> *It's often said that . . .*
>
> *For some people . . .*
>
> *That can vary according to the culture, but . . .*

Exam Practice Test 2 | Speaking Parts 1-3

Speaking Part 1

The examiner will start by introducing him / herself and checking your identity. He or she will then ask you some questions about yourself.

> *Let's talk about where you live. Do you live in a house or an apartment?*
>
> *How long have you been living in this house / apartment?*
>
> *What do you like about living in this house / apartment?*
>
> *Do you think you will move to another place in the future?*

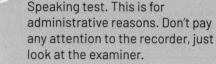

TIP The examiner will record the Speaking test. This is for administrative reasons. Don't pay any attention to the recorder, just look at the examiner.

The examiner will then ask you some questions about one or two other topics, for example:

> *Let's talk about the weather. What kind of weather did you like best when you were a child?*
>
> *Does the weather ever affect your mood?*
>
> *What is the best weather for studying or working?*
>
> *Would you like to live in a country that has very hot or very cold weather?*

TIP If you can't think of a good example from your own life, imagine a situation that is easy to talk about.

Speaking Part 2

The examiner will give you a topic like the one below and some paper and a pencil.

The examiner will say:

I'm going to give you a topic and I'd like you to talk about it for one to two minutes. Before you talk, you'll have one minute to think about what you're going to say. You can make some notes if you wish.   [1 minute]

All right? Remember you have one to two minutes for this, so don't worry if I stop you. I'll tell you when the time is up. Can you start speaking now, please?

Describe a time when you had a problem and someone helped you.

> *You should say:*
> > *what the problem was*
> > *who the person was who helped you*
> > *what this person did to help you*

and explain how you felt when this person helped you.

TIP Remember to speak clearly, not too quickly and not too slowly. You will receive a mark for pronunciation and, in particular, how easy it is for the examiner to understand you.

The examiner may ask one or two rounding-off questions when you have finished your talk, for example:

> *Did you tell your friends about this person who helped you?*
> *Do you often help other people who have problems?*

Speaking Part 3

The examiner will ask some general questions connected to the topic in Part 2.

The examiner will say, for example:

TIP You can also ask the examiner to repeat or rephrase a question if you're not sure that you've understood all of it. This won't affect your marks.

> *We've been talking about a time when you had a problem and someone helped you. I'd like to discuss with you one or two more general questions relating to this. First, let's consider helping in the home.*
>
> *What can children do to help in the home? How can parents encourage their children to help with daily tasks?*
>
> *Let's talk about helping in the local community now.*
>
> *Do you think people help their neighbours enough nowadays?*
>
> *Finally, let's talk about helping internationally.*
>
> *Do you agree that everyone should contribute to international charities?*

Exam Practice Test 3   Listening Part 1

🎧 **Questions 1–10**

18   *Complete the notes below.*

Write **ONE WORD AND / OR A NUMBER** for each answer.

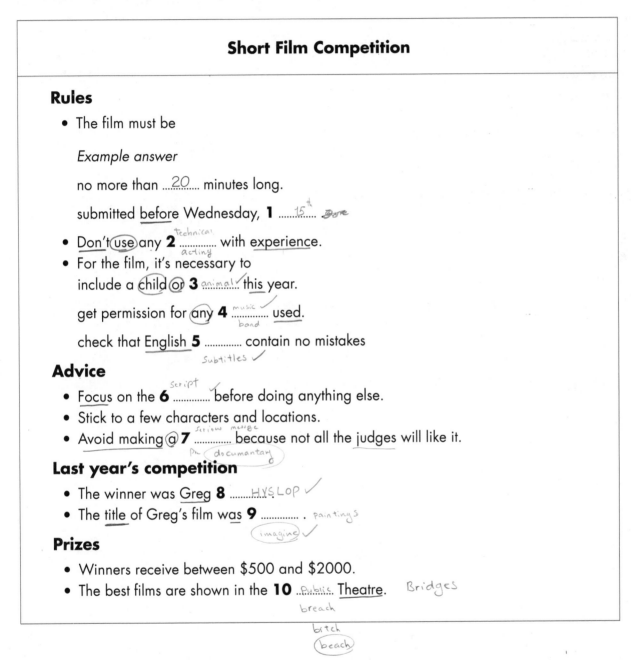

Short Film Competition

Rules

- The film must be

  Example answer

  no more than ....20.... minutes long.

  submitted <u>before</u> Wednesday, **1** ......15th.... ~~June~~

- Don't (use) any **2** ....(*technical / acting*) with <u>experience</u>.
- For the film, it's necessary to

  include a (child or) **3** ...*animal*... this year.

  get permission for (any) **4** ...*music / band*... used.

  check that English **5** .... contain no mistakes

  subtitles ✓

Advice

- <u>Focus</u> on the **6** ...*script*... before doing anything else.
- Stick to a few characters and locations.
- <u>Avoid</u> making (a) **7** ...*serious message*... because not all the <u>judges</u> will like it.

  Ph. (*documentary*)

Last year's competition

- The winner was <u>Greg</u> **8** ......HYSLOP ✓
- The title of Greg's film <u>was</u> **9** .... *paintings*

  (imagine) ✓

Prizes

- Winners receive between $500 and $2000.
- The best films are shown in the **10** ...*Public*... <u>Theatre</u>.   *Bridges*

  breach

  birch

  (*beach*)

Questions 11–12

19

*Choose **TWO** letters **A–E**.*

*Which **TWO** tasks will volunteers be required to do at Eskdale Wood?*

- **A** fix fences
- **B** remove branches
- **C** collect litter
- **D** build bird boxes
- **E** cut down trees

Questions 13–14

*Choose **TWO** letters **A–E**.*

*Which **TWO** things must volunteers bring with them?*

- **A** gloves
- **B** tools
- **C** snacks
- **D** sunscreen
- **E** boots

Questions 15–20

Complete the flow-chart below.

*Choose **SIX** answers from the box and write the correct letter, **A–H**, next to **Questions 15–20**.*

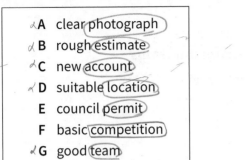

A clear photograph
B rough estimate
C new account
D suitable location
E council permit
F basic competition
G good team
H visual guide

To Take Part in the Bird Count

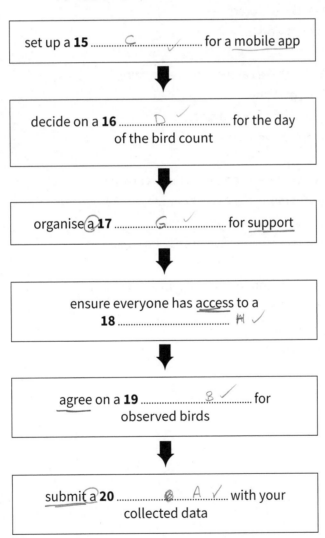

set up a **15** .... C .... for a mobile app

↓

decide on a **16** .... D .... for the day
of the bird count

↓

organise a **17** .... G .... for support

↓

ensure everyone has access to a
18 .... H ....

↓

agree on a **19** .... B .... for
observed birds

↓

submit a **20** .... A .... with your
collected data

🎧 **Questions 21–25**

20

*Choose the correct letter, **A**, **B** or **C**.*

Presentation on restoring and reproducing paintings

21 The students agree that the introduction to their presentation should include

   A reasons why paintings need to be restored.

   B examples of poor restoration work.

   C a general description of what restoration involves.

22 When the students visited the museum, they were surprised by

   A the time it took to restore a single painting.

   B the academic backgrounds of the restorers.

   C the materials used in restoration work.

23 What does Oliver say would put him off a career in art restoration?

   A the reaction of the owners of a painting

   B the possibility of working in dangerous conditions

   C the requirement to be able to draw very well

24 What do the students agree about the restored Dutch landscape painting?

   A It shows how taste in art varies amongst different people.

   B It is an example of a work that was once undervalued.

   C It demonstrates how cleaning techniques have greatly improved.

25 What is Oliver's attitude to the digital reproduction of famous paintings?

   A It requires a great deal of skill.

   B There is something dishonest about it.

   C It makes art accessible to more people.

Questions 26–30

What challenge did the Factum Arte team face with reproducing the following paintings?

*Choose **FIVE** answers from the box and write the correct letter, **A–G**, next to **Questions 26–30**.*

> **Challenges the Factum Arte team faced**
> **A** they only had a photo of a badly restored version of the painting
> **B** they needed to see under the damaged surface of the painting
> ✓**C** they had to get permission to analyse a very similar painting
> **D** they had to rely on similar drawings of the same subject
> **E** they had to negotiate with relations of the original artist
> **F** they were unable to view other examples of the artist's work
> **G** they had only limited time to reproduce the painting

Paintings the team wanted to reproduce

26 *Six Sunflowers* .... C ✓ A ask gau.

27 *The Concert* .... D ... B F — A

28 *Portrait of Sir Winston Churchill* .... E —— D

29 *The Water Lilies* .... B ✓

30 *Myrto* .... F ✓

Questions 31–40

21

Complete the notes below.

Write **ONE WORD ONLY** *for each answer.*

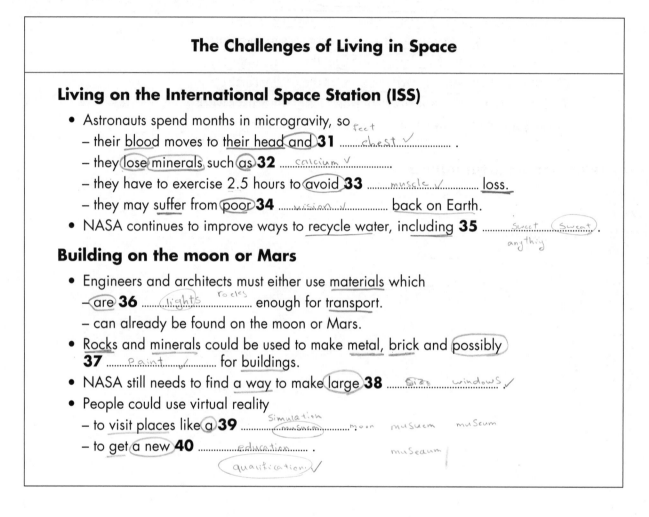

The Challenges of Living in Space

Living on the International Space Station (ISS)

- Astronauts spend months in microgravity, so ~~feet~~
  - their blood moves to their head and **31** ......chest..✓...... .
  - they (lose minerals) such (as) **32** ......calcium ✓......
  - they have to exercise 2.5 hours to (avoid) **33** ......muscle ✓...... loss.
  - they may suffer from (poor) **34** ......vision ✓...... back on Earth.
- NASA continues to improve ways to recycle water, including **35** ......sweat (sweat)......
  anything

Building on the moon or Mars

- Engineers and architects must either use materials which
  - (are) **36** ......lights...... ~~rocks~~ enough for transport.
  - can already be found on the moon or Mars.
- Rocks and minerals could be used to make metal, brick and (possibly)
  37 ......paint..✓...... for buildings.
- NASA still needs to find a way to make (large) **38** ......size windows ✓......
- People could use virtual reality
  - to visit places like (a) **39** ......simulation museum...... moon   museum   museum
  - to get (a) new **40** ......education...... .   museum ✓
    (qualification ✓)

*You should spend about 20 minutes on **Questions 1–14**, which are based on Reading Passage 1 below.*

*Read the text below and answer **Questions 1–7**.*

Pinehaven apartments
Rules for residents: Communal areas

Rooftop area

The rooftop is a shared space for everyone's enjoyment, so please leave it how you find it. If inviting more than five guests from outside the complex, please book a section of the rooftop ahead of time; the booking form is on the door of the utilities room. Please note that barbecues are used on a first-come-first-served basis. Please also leave them as you find them.

We ask that you are considerate of fellow residents and neighbours and keep noise levels down after 9 p.m. on weeknights.

While the janitor looks after the general maintenance of the area, it is not the job of the janitor to clean up after gatherings, so please make sure any garbage is removed from the rooftop and put in the bins on the ground floor.

Any breakage of communal property must be reported immediately and paid for.

The rooftop is closed from 10 p.m. Sunday to Thursday and 12 a.m. on Friday and Saturday.

Laundry

There are six washing machines and two dryers in the laundry. These cannot be booked in advance. If you leave your washing unattended after a cycle, note that it may be removed so others can use the machines.

Please notify the janitor immediately of any maintenance issues with the machines.

Elevators and stairwells

Be aware that our two elevators and three stairwells are communal areas; do not leave any items in these areas for any reason whatsoever. Elevators are in constant use at weekends so special arrangements need to be made if removalists need elevator access. Please contact management 24 hours in advance to reserve one if this is the case. If stairs are to be used when moving furniture, please use the West stairwell as the South stairwell is narrower and the North stairwell needs to be clear in case of emergencies.

Questions 1–7

Do the following statements agree with the information given Reading Passage 1?

In boxes 1–7 on your answer sheet, write

> **TRUE**   *if the statement agrees with the information*
> **FALSE**   *if the statement contradicts the information*
> **NOT GIVEN**   *if there is no information on this*

1   Barbecues on the rooftop area must be reserved in advance. NG   T
2   Rubbish from rooftop parties must be taken downstairs. T✓
3   The janitor should be notified of any damage to the rooftop area. F
4   You may use more than one washing machine at a time. NG ✓
5   The janitor checks the machines in the laundry regularly. NG
6   You have to book an elevator if you want to use it to move in or out on a weekend. T✓
7   The South stairwell has the best access for removalists. F✓

*Read the text below and answer **Questions 8–14**.*

Blakeville community college

A Barista course

Learn to make every coffee on a café menu. This course comprises eight hours of hands-on classroom delivery. Take our intensive course on Saturday 23 June or join our weekly two-hour sessions on Thursdays at 6:30 p.m.–8:30 p.m.

You'll learn to operate, clean and maintain a range of coffee machines, use a coffee grinder and present coffee like a professional.

Each student has their own machine – (max 12 in a class).

Cost: $290 ($10 off each when you book for two students).

B Leadlighting and stained glass

Learn the art of glass cutting and leadlighting as you make a project of your choice. Supplies are included in the cost and glass-cutters may be taken home, to be returned the following session. Runs Tuesdays 6:30 p.m.–9:00 p.m. from 24 June–22 July.

Cost: $320

C Sewing weekend course

Held over two days on the first weekend of every month (starting 28 June), this course is for those who want to make alterations to their garments or create new clothes and furnishings.

Your proficiency will be assessed by the instructor on the first morning, and you will receive instruction based on the stage you are at.

Machines and thread will be provided, but please bring your own fabric and pattern.

Cost: $250 for Saturday and Sunday.

D Drawing workshop

This course is a bridge for people who already like to draw to get to the next level. You'll be introduced to methods employed by contemporary artists using pencil, charcoal and ink. For the first session, please bring paper, pencil and eraser; you'll also need to purchase ink and charcoal pencils on the night. Held on Wednesday evenings between 7:00 p.m.–9:00 p.m., 25 June–23 July.

Cost: $180 plus incidentals

E Bicycle maintenance

A great starting point for those interested in bike care and repair. From fixing a puncture to adjusting brakes and gears, the team from BikeSmart will show you how. Saturday 10 a.m. to 12 p.m., 28 June and 5 July.

Cost: by donation

F Budgeting for beginners

This course will show you how to make a budget and stick to it. You'll learn to tailor your savings regime to your circumstances and you'll set and reach financial goals. These workshops run over three nights: Thursday 7:30 p.m.–9:00 p.m., starting 26 June. Bring a friend at no additional cost.

Cost: $90

Questions 8–14

*Look at the six descriptions of courses **A–F** in the text. For which courses are the following statements true?*

*Write the correct letter, **A–F**, in boxes 8–14 on your answer sheet.*

NB *You can use any letter more than once.*

8   You have to pay extra for materials. D ✓

9   The class is open to students of different levels of ability.

10   Two people can attend for the price of one. A F ✓

11   You can choose how much you want to pay for the class. E ✓

12   It is possible to borrow equipment. A B

13   You must have some experience in the skill being taught. C

14   A one-day course is offered. A ✓

You should spend about 20 minutes on **Questions 15–27**, which are based on Reading Passage 2.

Read Reading Passage 2 and answer **Questions 15–20**.

Setting up a home office, a how-to guide

Working from home is now an option in an increasing number of jobs, and many workers enjoy the flexibility this brings. However, not every home is automatically equipped to provide a workspace. Here are some tips for creating a professional home office, whether you are working for an employer or you have your own business:

- Establish the basic needs you have for your office. In most cases, you'll need a desk, adjustable chair and computer at least. Then you'll have an idea of how much space you'll need. You'll need a room away from noise and distractions and, if possible, it will be separate from communal areas with a closing door. Even if you don't share your home with others, it's a good idea to have a physical division between your home and work life.

- Maintaining a professional office means you'll need to be well-organised. Not only will you require space to spread out and work, you should allocate plenty of room for storage of files and supplies. You might have to store files in another room but, bear in mind that anything you use on a regular basis should be accessible.

- Getting the basics right is crucial: quality ergonomic furniture will ultimately save you money on treatment for physical problems caused by bad posture. While it can be tempting to skimp on key pieces and splurge on non-essentials like desk ornaments, it is far more important to have a reliable phone and computer, a fast internet connection and a chair that will support your lower back.

- Don't forget to hang a clock on the wall or put one on your desk where you can see it. It's easy to lose track of time when you're working from home and you might find yourself working for hours on end without a break. Conversely, you might feel it's time for a break before it actually is. You'll find you are far more efficient if you can set hours and stick to them. You'll stay more focused and clients will appreciate knowing when you can be reached.

- It is stipulated in health and safety policies of most workplaces that a first-aid kit should be provided, and this is best practice in the home office too. Ventilation, whether natural or artificial, must be adequate and the work area should be clear of obstructions.

Questions 15–20

Complete the sentences below.

*Choose **ONE WORD ONLY** from the text for each answer.*

Write the words in boxes 15–20 on your answer sheet.

15 Ideally, the office space in your home should be in a .... room.

16 Consider the need for .... as well as workspace.

17 Spend your budget on good equipment rather than unnecessary items, such as ....

18 Ensure a .... is visible from where you will be working.

19 Having regular office hours will be helpful for your ....

20 In terms of health and safety, it is important that there is enough ....

Read Reading Passage 2 below and answer **Questions 21–27**.

How to motivate your sales team: a guide for managers

Motivation is one of the most important ingredients of continued sales success over time. As a manager, you need to motivate your people as individuals and also as a team.

The foundation of motivation is trust. If your salespeople don't believe you have their best interests at heart, they won't be driven to put in their best effort at work. Take the time to find out their goals and the challenges they face in pursuing these goals.

The best way to find out what motivates your workers may simply be to ask them. Have them explain to you what management style they respond best to – some people need almost constant guidance while others like to be left to their own devices for most of the time. Ask them about the best times of the day or week to have meetings; although it may not always be possible, accommodate them when you can.

An often-overlooked factor is when and how to give feedback. Some need this – whether positive or negative – on a daily basis, while others would rather it was saved for more formal appraisals.

There are also some very tangible changes that may have an instant effect; these relate to the health and comfort of the workers. Ensure that they have time to recharge on their breaks and, if you can afford it, provide some nutritious, energy-giving snacks in the lunchroom. Some employers offer their workers a free or discounted membership at a gym and report that this pays for itself in healthy, motivated employees.

It's always worth remembering that people are motivated in different ways. The most commonly exploited motivator is money, whether it's a raise, bonus or commission, but that's not the only way of getting the best from your staff. Some thrive on competition, within or between teams. Others need acknowledgement for a job well done. Groups often respond positively to a chance to get out of the work environment, perhaps for social occasions or to attend sports events. Find what works for your sales people.

There are cases when workers are experiencing a slump and are not performing well. They may not rise to the challenge of working towards something they believe to be out of their reach. If this is the case, link their incentive to their improvement, rather than performance as measured against others.

Complete the notes below.

Choose **NO MORE THAN TWO WORDS** from the text for each answer.

Write your answers in boxes 21–27 on your answer sheet.

Motivating staff

General principles:
– <u>motivation</u> can't exist without **21** ...effort....

– manager must understand workers' goals, challenges

Ask workers:
– what **22** ...management style... they prefer ✓

– when they want meetings

– how often they need **23** ...feedback... ✓

Meet physical needs:
– adequate breaks

– healthy food

– access to a **24** ...gym... ✓

Examples of motivators:
– money

– **25** ...competition... with colleagues ✓

– praise / recognition

– outings such as parties and **26** ...sports events... ✓

Poor performers:
– offer rewards based on **27** ...incentive (improve...

You should spend about 20 minutes on **Questions 28–40**, which are based on Reading Passage 3.

Questions 28–32

Reading Passage 3 has five sections **A–E.**

Choose the correct heading for each section, **A–E**, from the list of headings below.

Write the correct number, **i–viii**, in boxes 28–32 on your answer sheet.

NB you can use any letter more than once.

✓28   Section **A**

✓29   Section **B**

·30   Section **C**

✓31   Section **D**

✓32   Section **E**

List of Headings

i   How do wallabies interact with other species?

ii   What is being done to protect wallabies? E

iii   What are the threats to the wallaby population? D

iv   How much contact do wallabies have with their offspring and with each other?

✓ v   What are the distinctive features of wallabies? A

vi   How do wallabies behave when in groups? C

✓ vii Where can wallabies be found? B

viii What kinds of wallaby are suited to specific environments?

The wallaby

Wallabies are small to medium-sized marsupials that inhabit the Australian continent and its surrounding islands. The word *wallaby* comes from the indigenous Australian language.

A

While the largest wallabies can measure 6 feet from head to tail, as big or bigger than some kangaroos, most species of wallaby are smaller than kangaroos. The smallest are around 12 inches when fully-grown. They have an upright posture supported by two disproportionately large hind legs and feet, small forelimbs and a large thick tail. Wallabies have strong hind legs that enable them to travel at speed; their sizeable Achilles tendons assist them in hopping. Besides hopping, the hind legs can also be used to deliver hard kicks to other wallabies. Their tails are not able to grip but are essential in that they provide balance when a wallaby is stationary or in motion.

Because wallabies are herbivores, they have a large jaw to allow them to chew grass and plants. This accounts for their elongated faces. One distinction between a wallaby and a kangaroo is the teeth: wallabies have flat molars at the back, while kangaroos' back teeth are curved.

B

Wallabies generally prefer bushy or rugged areas in remote locations of Australia, rather than the open arid plains that kangaroos prefer. Some smaller wallabies, such as pademelons, live in the forest. Often wallabies are named for the type of area where they reside, e.g. shrub wallabies, brush wallabies and rock wallabies.

From 1858 until 1870, about 12 species of marsupial were taken from Australia and liberated in New Zealand, but only the brush-tailed opossum and the wallabies adapted successfully to the new land. Inadequate early accounts of which exact species were introduced and where they were initially taken from, mean that there is still confusion with regards to which species of wallaby are actually present in New Zealand today.

In 1896, the acclaimed Australian painter Frederick McCubbin painted *On the wallaby track*, showing a family in the bush without a home, the woman with a child on her lap and the man boiling water for tea. The painting's title derives from the Australian colloquial term 'on the wallaby track' describing the wandering rural workers who moved from place to place for work and alluding to the nomadic tendency of wallabies.

C

In terms of their young, like all marsupials, wallabies are born at an early stage of development. Young wallabies, like young kangaroos, are called a *joey*. As soon as they are born, they crawl into their mothers' pouches and stay there, generally for around two months. At first, the joey spends varying lengths of time out of the pouch, grazing and acquiring vital survival skills. When it needs to sleep or it feels it is in danger; however, the joey will return to the pouch. In some species, joeys stay in the pouch for up to a year or until the next joey is born. However, for most wallabies the young are thought to be independent by 9 months.

There is significant variation when it comes to the daily habits of wallabies. The larger wallaby species tend to be diurnal (mostly active throughout the day) and live in mobs, or groups, whereas smaller species are generally nocturnal (active at night) and solitary.

D

There are animals that are native to Australia that have always hunted the wallaby; these include dingoes, wedge-tailed eagles and Tasmanian devils. However, it is species that were brought to Australia by settlers that have posed more danger. Foxes, cats and dogs have all taken their toll on wallaby numbers, as have herbivores like rabbits, sheep, goats and cattle that compete with wallabies for food. However, it is human activity that has had the most impact; land clearing and burning of bushlands have left great numbers of wallabies effectively homeless and without a source of food.

E

Four species of wallaby have already gone extinct. There are others that are classified as *vulnerable* or *endangered*, which means that they face a high or very high risk of extinction in the wild. Measures are being taken to help particular species, including conserving their habitats and breeding them in captivity, so they may be reintroduced into the wild at a later point when conditions are favourable.

While wallabies are considered by some farmers to be a pest, efforts are being made by the Australian Society for Kangaroos to stop farmers culling kangaroos and wallabies. Instead they advocate that they should be captured and relocated.

Questions 33–36

Label the diagram below.

*Choose **ONE WORD ONLY** from the Reading Passage for each answer.*

Write your answers in boxes 33–36 on your answer sheet.

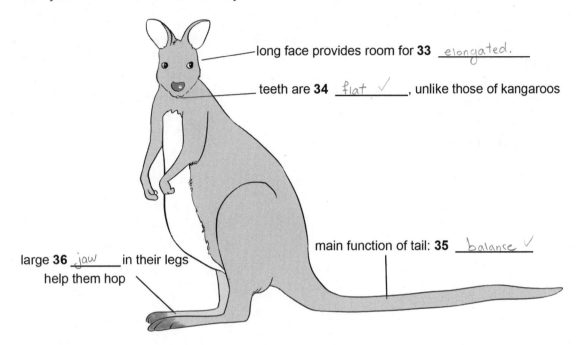

long face provides room for **33** _elongated._

teeth are **34** _flat_ ✓, unlike those of kangaroos

main function of tail: **35** _balance_ ✓

large **36** _jaw_ in their legs help them hop

Questions 37–40

*Write the correct letter, **A, B, C** or **D**, in boxes 37–40 on your answer sheet*

37 Where do wallabies tend to live?

   A in places inhabited by similar animals, such as kangaroos

   B in areas where bigger species cannot steal their food ✓

   C in dry areas with a minimum of vegetation

   D in wild places that are far away from humans

38 There is debate about which species of wallaby are present in New Zealand because

   A some seem to have disappeared since they were introduced.

   B records from the time they were introduced are incomplete.

   C they are sometimes mistaken for a type of possum.

   D they are shy creatures that avoid human contact.

39 'On the wallaby track' refers to people who ✓

   A travel around without a fixed home.

   B live in areas where wallabies can be found.

   C follow the trails of wallabies in order to hunt them.

   D make their home in a remote part of the country.

40 The greatest danger to the survival of wallabies is ✓

   A predator species that have been introduced to Australia.

   B animals that eat vegetation that wallabies need to survive.

   C native animals that have increased in numbers.

   D destruction of the places where they live.

Writing Task 1

> You should spend about 20 minutes on this task.
>
> **You recently made a journey by train. When you got on the train, you realised you had left a bag on the platform.**
>
> **Write a letter to the station manager. In your letter:**
> - **give details of where and when you left the bag**
> - **describe the bag and its contents**
> - **suggest how you could get the bag back**
>
> Write at least 150 words.
>
> You do **NOT** need to write any addresses.
>
> Begin your letter as follows:
>
> *Dear .... ,*

Writing Task 2

> You should spend about 40 minutes on this task.
>
> Write about the following topic:
>
> **Many people today choose to take part in extreme sports (e.g. skydiving, rock climbing).**
>
> **Why do you think people want to do these sports?**
>
> **Who do you think should pay if people injure themselves while doing an extreme sport?**
>
> Give reasons for your answer and include any relevant examples from your own knowledge or experience.
>
> Write at least 250 words.

Speaking Part 1

The examiner will start by introducing him/herself and checking your identity. He or she will then ask you some questions about yourself.

Let's talk about what you do. Do you work or are you a student?

Work

- *What job are you doing at the moment?*
- *What kind of job would you like to do in the future?*

Study

- *What subjects are you studying at the moment?*
- *What do you hope to do after you finish your studies?*

The examiner will then ask you some questions about one or two other topics, for example:

Let's talk about giving and receiving gifts.

- *Do you like choosing gifts for your friends?*
- *What was the best gift you ever received?*

Speaking Part 2

The examiner will give you a topic like the one below and some paper and a pencil.

The examiner will say:

I'm going to give you a topic and I'd like you to talk about it for one to two minutes. Before you talk, you'll have one minute to think about what you're going to say. You can make some notes if you wish.   [1 minute]

All right? Remember you have one to two minutes for this, so don't worry if I stop you. I'll tell you when the time is up. Can you start speaking now, please?

Describe a place in your country that you would really like to visit
   You should say:
      where this place is
      how long you would like to spend there
      who you would like to go with
   and explain why you would really like to visit this place in your country.

The examiner may ask one or two rounding-off questions when you have finished your talk, for example:

- *Do you think you will visit this place soon?*
- *Do you enjoy visiting different places?*

Speaking Part 3

The examiner will ask some general questions which are connected to the topic in Part 2. You will usually have to answer up to six questions.

The examiner will say, for example:

We've been talking about a place in your country that you would really like to visit. I'd like to discuss with you one or two more general questions relating to this. First, let's consider popular places to visit.

- *What are the most popular places to visit in your country?*
- *Why do many people like to visit historic buildings?*
- *Why is it hard sometimes to choose a place for a family group to visit?*

Let's talk about visiting other countries now.

- *What are the main benefits of visiting other countries?*
- *What preparations do people need to make before they visit another country?*

Finally, let's talk about the impact of tourism.

- *How can large numbers of tourists affect the environment in some places?*
- *What could be done to reduce the impact of mass tourism?*

Questions 1–10

22

Complete the notes below.

*Write **NO MORE THAN TWO WORDS AND / OR A NUMBER** for each answer.*

Island Transport		
Vehicles	**Cost**	**Comments**
Example Motor scooter	**1** $ .... per day 50.50 15. (49.99)	• fun to ride • they provide helmets and **2** ......gloves ✓ • don't ride on **3** ...BATTENBU.. Road BATTEN BUDG
Economy car	$87.80 per day	• four doors, five passengers • can drive on all the roads and to **4** ...greenbay... for a swim Island. • no **5** ...air conditioning... in the Economy car
E-Bike	**6** $ .... per day 59. (52.20) ✓	• battery is not very **7** ...heavy... • a quality bike with two good **8** ...brck... Padstates • a map and **9** ...lads... are provided • no **10** ...license... is needed

Questions 11–15

23

*Choose the correct letter, **A**, **B** or **C**.*

The Community Garden

11 What was recently discovered at this site?

A a written text about the area

B various tools used for farming

C some drawings showing the garden

12 This location is good for gardening because

A the weather is warm.

B there is enough water.

C it is protected from the wind.

13 In 1860, what was built on this site?

A a medical centre

B a type of factory

C a base for soldiers

14 Today, the fruit and vegetables from the gardens

A are sold to businesses in the area.

B are given to certain local people.

C are used by those who work in the garden.

15 The local college now uses the gardens

A as a location for scientific research.

B for educating the wider community.

C to teach its students gardening skills.

Questions 16–20

Label the map below.

*Write the correct letter, **A–H**, next to **Questions 16–20**.*

The Community Garden

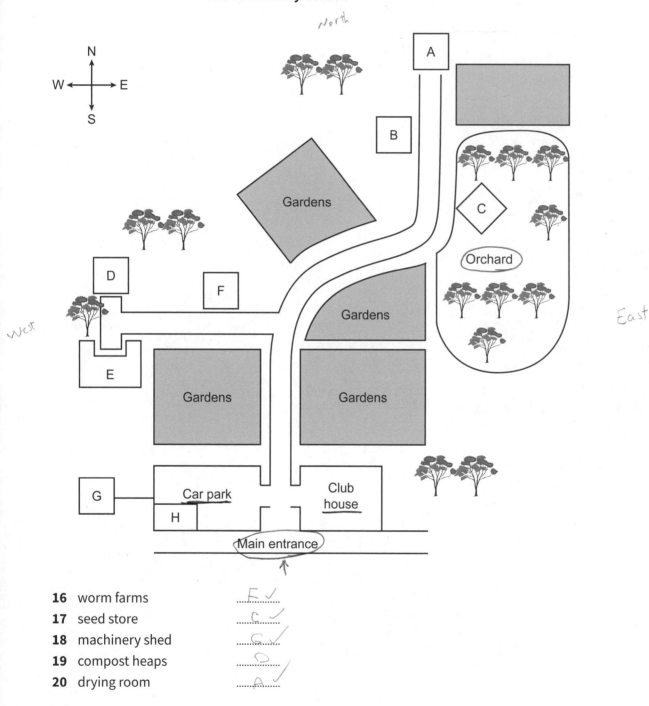

16 worm farms   E ✓

17 seed store   C ✓

18 machinery shed   G ✓

19 compost heaps   D ✓

20 drying room   A ✓

Questions 21–25

Write the correct letter, A, B or C, next to Questions 21–25.

The Benefits of Playing Video Games

21 According to Alya and Jason, Dr Franklin showed that video games have

   A been used in therapy for a long time.

   B only a limited number of uses in therapy.

   C been accepted by most doctors working in therapy.

22 According to the students, what is the biggest advantage of games in therapy?

   A Some injuries occur less frequently.

   B Costs are lower than other treatments.

   C Patients work harder at their recovery.

23 When discussing the Singapore study, the students disagree about

   A the purpose of the research.

   B the methodology used in the research.

   C the conclusions reached by the researchers.

24 What impresses the students about the anxiety research?

   A the variety of games that were used

   B results were confirmed in another study

   C both patients and their families benefitted

25 The students agree that the Rhode Island research

   A provided reliable evidence.

   B has received widespread publicity.

   C has been criticised by some academics.

Questions 26–30

What opinion do the students express about each research study?

*Choose FIVE answers from the box and write the correct letter, **A–G**, next to **Questions 26–30**.*

Opinions
A the finding may disappoint some businesses
B the finding contradicts other research
C the finding is relevant in particular countries
D the finding is not believable
E the finding is supported by various studies
F the finding is not a surprise
G the finding will become increasingly important

26 surgeon study .... C / E

27 vision study ...... B E E ✓

28 sport study . ... D ✓

29 ageing study .... G ✓

30 career study .... E ✓

Questions 31–40

Complete the notes below.

Write **ONE WORD ONLY** for each answer.

Traditional Polynesian Navigation

Introduction

- the islands of Polynesia are in the Pacific Ocean
- the Polynesian peoples originally migrated from **31** .... to the Pacific islands
  Asia / Americas / Eastern
- European explorers were impressed that Polynesian canoes were **32** ....strong faster.... than European ships

Equipment on ocean-going canoes

- paddles were used for **33** ....back.... *Propticu Steing*
- sails were made from the pandanus plant *buck bark*
- warm clothes were made from the **34** ....flexible.... of the paper mulberry tree
  water In trupic

How Polynesians navigated at sea

- they did not have the magnetic compass
- they remembered where stars rose and set by making up detailed **35** ....direction.... *Songs*
- when it was cloudy, they found the direction by using **36** ....stars.... *waves*

Finding new islands

- they could identify certain **37** ....birds.... *tectni* that only live near land
- close to land, they could read changes in the sea's **38** ....changes....

Recent history

- in 1976 the canoe *Hokule'a* sailed from Hawaii to Tahiti without **39** ....crowds.... *airplane*
- now replica traditional canoes have sailed across the Pacific and around the world
- as well as sailing, these voyages have created fresh interest in Polynesian culture, music and **40** ....languages....

You should spend about 20 minutes on **Questions 1–14**, which are based on Reading Passage 1. *12 min*

Read the text below and answer **Questions 1–7**.

Notice of public meeting: The M32 development

The Fortescue Neighbourhood Action Group is urging residents to attend a public meeting to hear the concerns of local residents and families of pupils from Fortescue Primary School about the approval of the final stage of the M32 motorway.

On 17 April, the Government approved Stage 3 of the M32 motorway development, which will affect the Fortescue area. It was not until ten days later that this approval was finally announced.

Date: May 5

Time: 6:30 p.m.

Location: Jarrah Community Hall, corner of Fortescue Road and Huxley Parade, Fortescue.

Speakers: Ann Banks (Local council)

Marcin Kowalski (Parents Association, Fortescue Primary)

Louise Chang (President, Conservation Volunteers)

45 minutes will be reserved for questions and public comment.

Community organisations successfully lobbied for more dedicated parks and for noise restrictions in Zone 1. The developers, BD Construction, acted on this due to objections from the community.
We have to keep up the pressure!

Points of concern

- In the first stage of the development, the majority of wildlife and birds in the area moved (or were moved by conservation groups) from Zone 1 to Zone 2. Now that Zone 2 is to be developed, no policy exists to assist these animals; they have little chance of finding an appropriate habitat nearby.
- It is unclear how the motorway will improve traffic on Packers Road.
- There has been no announcement about how to manage the traffic bottleneck in Bradford Street that will result from roadworks.
- Traffic jams / gridlock are anticipated on the arterial roads surrounding the entry point to the new section of motorway.
- The Environmental Impact Statement put out by BD Construction for Stage 3 does not specifically address the issue of noise and pollution in Hyde's Reserve.
- With Fortescue Primary School just 50 metres from the main construction site, school students will be subjected to years of dust and noise, and then by unfiltered emissions from vehicle exhaust pipes.

Come along and have your say!

Questions 1–7

Do the following statements agree with the information given in Reading Passage 1?

In boxes 1–7 on your answer sheet, write

> **TRUE**   *if the statement agrees with the information*
>
> **FALSE**   *if the statement contradicts the information*
>
> **NOT GIVEN** *if there is no information on this*

6 m.

1 Stage 3 of the development was made public as soon as it was approved. F
2 The developers responded to public complaints about Zone 1. T
3 The meeting will be led by a representative from the Parents Association. N G
4 There is a plan to safely relocate animals in Zone 2. F
5 Packers Road currently has more traffic problems than Bradford Street. P7B N G
6 The developers produced a document about the effects of the development on nature in the area. F
7 Children will be affected by the construction activities. T

Questions 8–14

*Read the text below and answer **Questions 8–14**.*

Concorde festival

● ● ●

Concorde Festival has always been a family affair and this year is no exception!

A

10:00–17:00 (all day)

Beats and bites food , music

Hamperdown Avenue will be transformed into an outdoor eatery. Come and sample delicacies from nearby restaurants including Georgio's Pizza, Al Basha Kebab House and Texas Fry-Up. Lively bands, including international act Firehouse will entertain throughout the day.

Pedestrian zone, Hamperdown Ave

B

10:00–11:30

Little farmers

Home Gardening for Kids
Presented by East City Farms
Located in the Eco Village (south-west corner of Hamperdown Park)

7th Heaven hip-hop troupe

Come and see students from East Concorde Middle School show you their moves!
Main Stage

C

10:30–16:00

Hamperdown brew zone

If the excitement of the festival becomes too much, have a break in the chill-out zone. We have set up bean-bags, picnic blankets and a drinks stand run by local coffee house, Hamperdown Brew, under the trees along the eastern side of Hamperdown Park. Vocal acts, such as Joss and Bill, along with other graduates from the Concorde School of Music, will entertain throughout the day. Pets welcome.

local singer
Rest

D

11:00–12:00

Poster making

Celebrating the things we love about Concorde! Unleash your creativity and maybe win book vouchers, (ages 5–10)
Located in the Kids Workshop Area
Presented by Hamperdown Library

E

12:00–13:00

Make it yourself

Alex Mastroianni & Sabine Deleflie, Authors of *Make it yourself*, present Salads & Pickles Talk and Demonstration. Learn to make your own pickles with what's in your fridge or garden.

Sanderson Stage

F

13:00–14:00

Hamperdown hounds

The annual dog parade and 'dress-up-the-dog' contest has become a much-awaited event. Doggie treats will be awarded to winners.

Northern perimeter of Hamperdown Park.

G

14:00–15:30

Cartooning and colouring-in activities for kids

Located in the Kids Workshop Area
Presented and guided by cartoonist and illustrator Charlotte Mantel

Questions 8–14

*Look at the seven descriptions of events **A–G**.*

For which events are the following statements true?

*Write the correct letter, **A–G**, in boxes 8–14 on your answer sheet.*

NB *You may use any letter more than once.*

8   You can see a presentation about preparing food. E

9   You can watch a group of young people dancing. B

10   Children can draw with the help of an expert. G

11   You can listen to local singers. C

12   There are prizes for children. D

13   There are activities for pets. F

14   There is a place to take a rest. C

You should spend about 20 minutes on **Questions 15–27**, which are based on the two texts below.

Read the text below and answer **Questions 15–21**.

Memo: To all key holders and persons responsible for locking up

Head office is streamlining procedures for the safety and security of employees, cash and stock. Below is the procedure for closing the Vern's Clothing Warehouse. Please follow these steps in all branches.

Vern's Clothing Warehouse: Procedure for closing the shop

Tasks:

One hour before the store closes

- Restock shelves, making a note of anything that needs to be ordered.
- Assign cleaning duties to staff members.
- Take defective returned merchandise to the back room to be processed / sent to warehouse.
- Put all non-defective returned merchandise back on shelves.
- Check window display and wheel the external sale table back inside.

Closing the shop

- Walk the floor, double-checking for any remaining customers. Be sure to check the fitting rooms, pulling back curtains as you go.
- Lock the side door with the key and bolt it at both top and bottom.
- Lock the automatic door (main entry) by pushing the red button to the left of the door.
- Observe departing employees, ensuring that all merchandise being taken has been paid for.
- No friends are allowed on the premises at closing time. Please have them wait outside.

Handling registers and money

- Close the cash register and lock the till.
- Count cash away from registers so that it will not be visible to people who might be able to view the activity from outside the store through windows. The back office is the best place for counting money.
- Place the till tape, daily report and all money in the safe there.
- Two people must always be present when the safe is open and money is being counted, so always do this in the presence of a co-worker.
- Leave register drawers open to better protect point of sale terminals in the event of a break-in because burglars are likely to damage a register if trying to gain access.
- Leave the appropriate lighting on – a sign near the main switch panel indicates which lights are not to be turned off.
- Activate the burglar alarm to the left of the front entrance by typing the code into the pad followed by the # key. This will give you 90 seconds to lock up and leave.
- Leave the key with security if you are not rostered on the following day.

Questions 15–21

Complete the flow-chart below.

*Choose **NO MORE THAN TWO WORDS** from the text for each answer.*

Write your answers in boxes 15–21 on your answer sheet.

Vern's Clothing Warehouse: Procedure for closing the shop

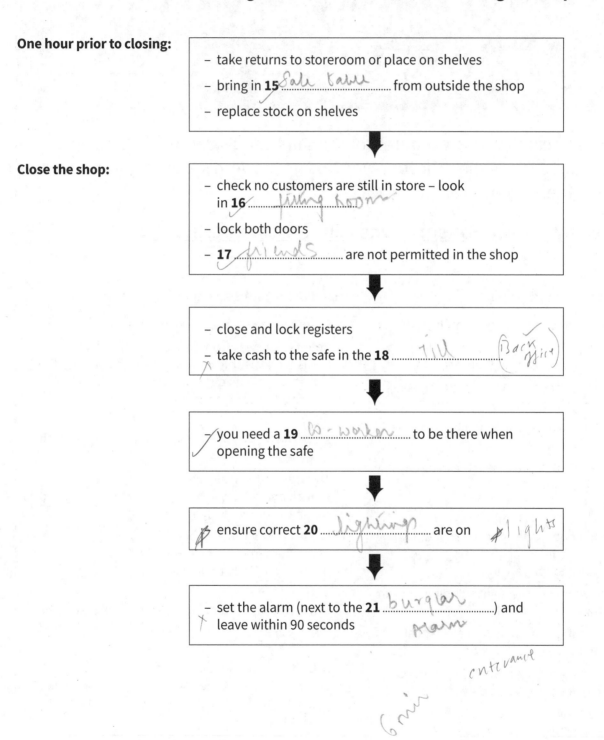

One hour prior to closing:

- take returns to storeroom or place on shelves
- bring in **15** ~~Sale table~~ from outside the shop
- replace stock on shelves

Close the shop:

- check no customers are still in store – look in **16** ~~fitting room~~
- lock both doors
- **17** ~~friends~~ are not permitted in the shop

- close and lock registers
- take cash to the safe in the **18** ~~Till~~ (Back office)

- you need a **19** ~~co-worker~~ to be there when opening the safe

- ensure correct **20** ~~lightings~~ are on *lights*

- set the alarm (next to the **21** ~~burglar~~) and leave within 90 seconds *alarm*

entrance

The Heritage Hotel

Uniform policy

The Heritage Hotel is committed to dress standards that will enhance its corporate image, and it is essential that grooming and presentation be of the highest standard at all times.

Employees are required to maintain a neat, clean, well-groomed appearance. The discretion of what constitutes acceptable grooming rests with the company.

Uniform specifications

- Staff who have contact with customers (e.g. reception and management) are to wear either a white or black shirt with a pocket that displays the Heritage Hotel insignia (employees are issued one shirt in each colour). These staff members will be issued with a burgundy Heritage Hotel jacket, to be worn with the regulation black skirt or trousers, also provided by the Hotel.

- Those working back-of-house in maintenance and housekeeping roles will be provided with two white Bob Charles shirts with the Hotel insignia on the front. Trousers or a skirt in navy blue will also be issued by the Hotel.

- Shoes are to be comfortable and clean. They should be black and with a heel of less than 3cm. For safety reasons, no open-toed shoes are permitted.

- Anyone employed by the Heritage Hotel is to ensure their name badge is visible at all times during their shift.

Care of uniform

- The hotel issues complete uniforms to all staff, which are signed for on commencement of employment and must be returned when leaving the company.

- The hotel uniform, whether for management / reception or maintenance / housekeeping should always be freshly pressed with no stains, loose threads or missing buttons.

- Those working as managers or at reception may store their uniform in the locker in the office to the rear of reception and keep the jacket there during the shift if it is not being worn. It can be laundered when necessary in the hotel laundry.

- Those working in maintenance and housekeeping may also have their uniform laundered. Uniforms can be placed in the laundry basket in the ground-floor staffroom and picked up from the shelf in the same room for the next shift. It must be recorded on the wall chart when an item is dropped off or collected.

- If the management / reception uniform is torn, please take it directly to Ms Nichols in the laundry. Maintenance / housekeeping staff should notify their team leader if their uniform needs mending or replacing.

Questions 22–27

Complete the table below.

Write **NO MORE THAN TWO WORDS** from the text for each answer.

Write your answers in boxes 22–27 on your answer sheet.

The Heritage Hotel

Uniform policy			
	Management / Reception		**Housekeeping / Maintenance**
Top	– shirt (white or black) with logo on 22 ..~~pocket~~.. hotel jacket		– white Bob Charles shirt with company logo
Trousers / skirt	– colour: black – supplied and fitted by hotel		– colour: 23 *Navy blue*
Shoes	– must not be 24 *open toed*	*Not more than 3cm*	
25 *Name badge*	– must be worn by all staff members while at work		
Storage and laundering of uniform	– keep in locker behind reception		– sign for clean uniform in 26 *wall chart* *(staff room)*
Damaged uniform	– take to Ms Nichols (laundry)		– report to 27 *Team leader*

10 min

You should spend about 20 minutes on **Questions 28–40**, which are based on Reading Passage 3.
Read the text below and answer **Questions 28–40**.

Urban fish farming

New initiatives are making the widespread farming of fish in cities a real possibility.

It is estimated that the world's population will have reached 8 billion people by the year 2030, which is a matter of concern in terms of the global food supply. It is thought that by then, only 38% of seafood consumed will come from wild sea life, meaning that the rest will be sourced from fish farming. Using a system called aquaponics however, it is possible to cultivate both fish and produce (e.g. vegetables) in a closed-loop system. The fish waste fertilises the plants and the plants purify the water making it habitable for the fish. This idea has been used in fish farming for years; recently however, there have been some initiatives that are using aquaponics in a city environment.

Many offshore fish farms are experiencing a number of issues. Often, the waters where they are located are becoming less attractive as habitats because the water is getting warmer and, therefore, has higher levels of acidity. In addition to this, this type of farming often relies on antibiotics and pesticides. Leftover fish waste can pollute the area and have a negative effect on other species. These reasons have led researchers and entrepreneurs to investigate alternative ways of farming fish.

New York scientist Martin Schreibman keeps fish in large tanks in his laboratory – a very different set-up from a conventional fish farm or, for that matter, from a natural ecosystem. He has been working on a system that eliminates the use of chemicals in the rearing of the fish. This system filters water from the tap and removes waste created by the fish. No antibiotics or pesticides are added but he is able to control the temperature of the water and has had particular success with tilapia fish, which he says are ideal for research thanks to their resilience. By making his recirculation system sufficiently compact that it can be operated using the city water supply, Schreibman believes tanks like his could be used on city rooftops to provide residents with fish all year round.

The idea behind aquaponics is far from new. As far back as 1,000 BC farmers in China realised they were able to boost the yield from their rice paddies when they let fish swim in the water around the rice and fertilise the plants with their waste. Jason Green explains that his company, Edenworks, wants to adapt that early knowledge, which used an ecosystem that was already there, to the modern situation where the ecosystem can be separate and independent from the land. He notes that the challenge is to create soil that has the same richness and nutrient support as a natural system has.

In trying to recreate the right balance to produce delicious food, Edenworks monitors all conditions on the farms using sensors. The company has enlisted the help of professional chef and now Edenworks' Head of Product, Sam Yoo, to sample the food once it is harvested. Yoo uses his highly-trained palette to help quantify aspects of the food like flavour and texture.

One notable feature of Edenworks farms is that they use a vertical design. This enables them to grow up to six times as much produce in the same sized space as other systems. They do not use LED or fluorescent lights, preferring instead a solar design. Currently they sell produce and fish directly to restaurants, but Green explains Edenworks would like to get to a point where the aquaponic model of food production is integrated into building design from the start. He adds that besides providing food, a rooftop farm serves as a layer of insulation for the building, thus benefitting the occupants in additional ways.

There are undoubted benefits of urban farming for the environment. The average item in an American grocery story currently travels 1500 miles on its way to the shelf. Producing food in cities would not only vastly reduce the energy required for distribution but would also have a positive effect on how fresh and nutritious the fruits and vegetables in local communities are.

Neil Sims of Kampachi Farms has been deeply involved in the fish-farming industry, though off the coast of Hawaii rather than in cities. Sims and his colleagues have found that they have had to overcome the public perception of farmed fish or fish grown in a warehouse as being somehow inferior nutritionally. He acknowledges that some poorly-executed attempts at fish farming in the past may have made people sceptical but notes that the resistance should be countered with the possibility of a sustainable, healthy source of fish. As Sims points out, if the number of people on Earth approaches the expected 11 billion at the end of the century, there will simply not be enough fish to feed everyone. That is, of course, unless a new way of supplying fish is adopted.

Questions 28–32

Look at the following statements (**Questions 28–32**) and the list of people (**A–D**) below.

Match each statement with the correct person, **A, B, C** or **D**.

Write the correct letter, **A, B, C** or **D**, in boxes 28–32 on your answer sheet.

NB you may use any letter more than once.

28 He believes that traditional fishing will not keep pace with population growth.

29 He states that a particular type of fish is suited to being farmed.

30 He analyses the taste of food carefully.

31 He believes that no artificial substances need to be added to the water.

32 He found that some people are reluctant to embrace the idea of fish farming.

List of People

A Martin Schreibman

B Jason Green

C Sam Yoo

D Neil Sims

Questions 33–36

Choose the correct letter, **A, B, C** or **D**.

Write the correct letter in boxes 33–36 on your answer sheet.

33 One advantage of aquaponics mentioned in the first paragraph is that

    A people are quick to adopt it when they understand it.

    B plants and animals benefit from each other.

    C many cities are already equipped to put it into practice.

    D food can reach customers the same day it is harvested.

34 What problem with fish farming in the ocean is mentioned?

    A Fish farms are too far from the consumer.

    B Diseased fish are becoming immune to medicines used.

    C Conditions are becoming less favourable for some marine creatures.

    D Other marine species may interfere with fish being farmed.

35 A distinctive aspect of the fish farming done by Edenworks is that

    A they can maximise the use of space.

    B they produce higher quality fish than other companies.

    C they operate in taller buildings.

    D they make use of artificial lighting.

36 What does Green say about designing farms within buildings?

    A Urban architects have opposed these farms so far.

    B These farms may bring other advantages as well as providing food.

    C These farms should not be located too high up in the building.

    D These farms will work well in a limited set of conditions.

Questions 37–40

Complete the summary below.

*Choose **ONE WORD ONLY** from the text for each answer.*

Write your answers in boxes 37–40 on your answer sheet.

Bringing back an old concept

From 1,000 BC Chinese rice farmers made use of aquaponics, which helped them to increase their **37** yield. They allowed fish into the rice paddies and the **38** waste from the fish naturally enriched their crops. Edenworks is looking at ways to incorporate that idea, but with a system that is not connected to the **39** land. They are trying to find a way to produce food that tastes great by duplicating the qualities of **40** soil found in nature.

Nutrients – +

Exam Practice Test 4 | Writing Tasks 1–2

Writing Task 1

You should spend about 20 minutes on this task.

You recently took part in a training course. The organiser of the course has asked you for some feedback.

Write a letter to the organiser of the course. In your letter:
- *give details of the course you took part in*
- *say what you found useful on the course*
- *suggest ways the course could be improved*

Write at least 150 words.

You do **NOT** need to write any addresses.

Begin your letter as follows:

Dear ....,

Writing Task 2

You should spend about 40 minutes on this task.

Write about the following topic:

Many people today buy ready-made food rather than spending time cooking.

What do you think are the reasons for this?

Do you think the advantages of this development outweigh the disadvantages?

Give reasons for your answer and include any relevant examples from your own knowledge or experience.

Write at least 250 words.

Speaking Part 1

The examiner will start by introducing him / herself and checking your identity. He or she will then ask you some questions about yourself.

Let's talk about where you live.

- *Where is your home town/city?*
- *What's special about your home town/city?*
- *Would you like to change anything in your home town/city?*

The examiner will then ask you some questions about one or two other topics, for example:

Let's talk about parks and gardens.

- *How often did you go to a park when you were younger?*
- *Do you enjoy visiting parks now?*
- *Do you think your town/city has enough parks and gardens?*

Speaking Part 2

The examiner will give you a topic like the one below and some paper and a pencil.

The examiner will say:

I'm going to give you a topic and I'd like you to talk about it for one to two minutes. Before you talk, you'll have one minute to think about what you're going to say. You can make some notes if you wish. [1 minute]

All right? Remember you have one to two minutes for this, so don't worry if I stop you. I'll tell you when the time is up. Can you start speaking now please?

Describe the sport that you most like watching

You should say:

    what sport you most like watching

    where you watch this sport

    when you last watched this sport

and explain why you like watching this sport so much

The examiner may ask one or two rounding-off questions when you have finished your talk, for example:

- *Do your family also like watching this sport?*
- *Do you enjoy playing any sports?*

Speaking Part 3

The examiner will ask some general questions which are connected to the topic in Part 2. You will usually have to answer up to six questions.

The examiner will say, for example:

We've been talking about the sport that you most like watching. I'd like to discuss with you one or two more general questions relating to this. First, let's consider playing sports.

- *Which sports do many people enjoy playing in your country?*
- *What can people learn from playing team sports?*
- *Should all children learn to play sports at school? Why do you think that?*

Let's talk about professional sportspeople now.

- *Why do you think the top sportspeople are paid so much?*
- *What are the disadvantages of being a top sportsperson?*

Finally, let's talk about extreme sports.

- *Why are extreme sports growing in popularity today?*
- *Many people feel governments should ban the most dangerous extreme sports? Do you agree with that view?*

Questions 1–10

26

Complete the form below.

Write **ONE WORD AND / OR A NUMBER** for each answer.

INSURANCE CLAIM FORM

Example	
Client details	
Name:	**Greg** Williams

Policy reference: **1** .... 05.443 CHi 771 ✓

Address: **2** 102 ...Market.../...... Street, Northbridge

Phone number: **3** ....018.669 925 ✓

Description of damage

Date of incident: Sunday, 17ᵗʰ June

Cause of incident: the house was damaged during ⓐ**4** ......Storm...✓...

Items client is claiming for:

~~window~~

a pair of child's **5** ......glasses✓...

a new **6** ...~~dress~~ ~~cap~~ headphone (Carpet)✓

a torn **7** ......~~headPhone~~ Curb   carpent   carpet

repairs to the door of the **8** ....

garage ✓

Builder dealing with damage

Full name: Steven **9** ...Honeywell...   glassess

Client to send in photographs of damaged **10** ...fence✓... before building work starts

---

Questions 11–12

*Which **TWO** opportunities does the Young Explorer Programme offer to participants?*

*Choose **TWO** letters, **A–E**.*

A Improving negotiation skills

B Developing supportive relationships

C Acquiring a new physical skill

D Learning about environmental issues

E Competing for an award

Questions 13–14

*Which **TWO** subjects must groups study in their preliminary training?*

*Choose **TWO** letters, **A–E**.*

A Finding sources of water

B Operating cooking equipment

C Knowing how to follow a route

D Searching for safe things to eat

E Using wood to build shelters

Questions 15–20

What does the speaker say about each of the following tracks?

Write the correct letter A, B, C or D next to Questions 15–20.

Tracks

15 Northface   .... C ✓

16 Blue River   .... B ~~A~~ ✓

17 Pioneer   .... D. ✓

18 Edgewater   .... A ✓

19 Murray   .... B ✓

20 Lakeside   .... A ✓

A	It is likely to be busy.
B	It may be unsafe in places.
C	It is currently closed to the public.
D	It is divided into two sections.

Questions 21–26

28 *Write the correct letter, **A**, **B** or **C**, next to **Questions 21–26**.*

The Future of Work

21 Kiara and Finn agree that the articles they read on the future of work
   A mainly reflect the concerns of older employees.
   B refer to the end of a traditional career path.
   C tend to exaggerate the likely changes.

22 What point does Kiara make about the phrase 'job title'?
   A It is no longer relevant in modern times.
   B It shows colleagues how to interact with each other.
   C It will only apply to people higher up in an organisation.

23 What issue affecting young employees is Finn most concerned about?
   A lack of job security
   B income inequality
   C poor chances of promotion

24 What is Kiara's attitude towards the Richards-Greeves survey on work-life balance?
   A She thinks that the findings are predictable.
   B She is curious about the kind of work the interviewees do.
   C She believes it would be useful to know what the questions were.

25 Finn and Kiara agree that if employees are obliged to learn new skills,
   A they should learn ones which might be useful in another job.
   B they should not be forced to learn them in their own time.
   C they should receive better guidance from training departments.

26 When Finn talks about the impact of mobile technology, Kiara responds by
   A emphasising the possible disadvantages.
   B describing her personal experience.
   C mentioning groups who benefit most from devices.

Questions 27–30

28 What impact might Artificial Intelligence (AI) have on each of the following professions?

*Choose **FOUR** answers from the box and write the correct letter, **A–F**, next to **Questions 27–30**.*

Impact of Artificial Intelligence (AI)

A It will give them a greater sense of satisfaction.
B It will encourage them to compete with one another.
C It will reduce the level of stress they have.
D It may eventually lead to their jobs disappearing.
E It could prevent them from coming to harm.
F It will enable them to do tasks they have not trained for.

27 Architects .... A
28 Doctors .... D ... C
29 Lawyers C
30 Sports referees .... E

Questions 31–40

29

Complete the notes below.

Write ONE WORD ONLY for each answer.

The Klondike Gold Rush of Canada

The gold-seekers' journey to the Klondike river

- Many gold-seekers set off from Skagway in Alaska.
- The White Pass Trail was difficult because of rocks and **31** ...horse... along the way. *Progress*
- The Chilkoot Trail was very **32** ...speed... so it could take three months. *stip*
- On both trails, gold-seekers gave up because of starvation, disease and the fear of **33** ...journey... .
- At Lake Bennet, gold-seekers stayed in @ **34** ...boat... until spring arrived. *lake frozen*
- At Miles Canyon, it was necessary to hire an experienced **35** ...sailor... to continue the journey. *real seller*
- Gold-seekers finally reached Dawson and the Klondike river.

The equipment gold-seekers had to take

- The **36** ...police... provided gold-seekers with a list. *transport*
- The list included
    - clothes, e.g. boots, thick coats
    - tea and food such as **37** ...flour...
    - tools, e.g. rope and several **38** ...buckets...

People who became successful because of the gold rush

- Some business-minded people sold supplies or set up hotels.
- Jack London created a sense of **39** ...adventure... in his stories. *adventure* *Survive ride*
- Annie Hall Strong and Emma Kelly contributed to various **40** ...newspaper... in Canada and the US.

You should spend about 20 minutes on **Questions 1–14**, which are based on the two texts below.

Read the text below and answer **Questions 1–7**.

Product recall: Healthfast

A Healthfast Vitamins and Wellbeing wishes to inform its retailers and customers that foreign material has been found in some bottles and containers of its vitamins and supplements. These foreign items include sawdust, paint chips and metal shavings.

B Batches affected

You will find the batch number printed on the bottom of the jar or container.

Goodnight Formula3 P6617–P6628

Healthfast Diet Support tablets N5990– N5992

Anti-stress Formula DR5938– DR5941

C If the batch number has worn off or you have any queries relating to the recall, please call the dedicated hotline on 1800 98887777. Alternatively, our retailers have been briefed and are being regularly updated, so you may enquire at the outlet where the purchase was made.

D These products are available nationwide, but reports of faulty items have come from the Sussex Cove area, leading us to believe that they have been tampered with locally. However, in the interests of security, we urge all customers who have products from the list above to return them immediately, either to point of purchase or via post to head office (Freepost SU9877). If you have opened the bottle / container, please inspect and report any irregularities.

E Refunds

As the manufacturer, the health and safety of our customers is paramount. We will provide a refund for any unopened bottle or container from the list above, no questions asked. We will be inspecting these in order to continue to ascertain and monitor the situation.

F If you have consumed vitamins or supplements from the affected batches, we would be grateful if you could complete the attached survey and report the place of purchase of the product. Please note that our children's supplement range and Sportsboost vitamins have not been affected and do not need to be returned.

G Healthfast Vitamins and Wellbeing will pay a reward of up to $20,000 for information leading to the conviction of any person found guilty of tampering with its products. If you have such information, please contact Regina Giese, Customer Relations Manager, Healthfast Vitamins and Wellbeing, at rgiese@healthfast.co.

Questions 1–7

*The reading text above has seven sections, **A–G**.*

Which section mentions the following information?

*Write the correct letter, **A–G**, in boxes 1–7 on your answer sheet.*

NB *You may use any letter more than once.*

1 which exact products are being recalled

2 what the manufacturer will do with returned products

3 who to contact to find out more

4 what to do if you have bought a recalled product but have not used it

5 what the manufacturer is offering for details of the crime

6 where recalled products were sold

7 why the products are being recalled

*Read the text below and answer **Questions 8–14**.*

Taking a holiday in Canada – on a budget

Canada is often considered to be an expensive place to travel because of the climate, vast distances and high cost of domestic travel, but this doesn't have to be the case. Below are some tips to help plan a Canadian trip that won't break the bank.

Getting around

- Buses and trains in Canada are reliable but can be expensive and limit where you are able to go. One option for travelling between and within cities is a rideshare scheme. Locals with empty seats in their cars will take you from A to B for a fee.

- If you want to hire a car, don't assume you have to go with a big company. There are lesser-known companies that hire out older cars, which are still reliable. Either way, there are savings to be had when you book outside the peak months (May, June and September). Be aware of add-on costs, however. The base rate does not generally include car insurance or unlimited kilometres.

- If your dates are flexible, you may make great savings with a campervan relocation deal. These deals come up when a rental company needs a vehicle moved from one office to another one way for example, Halifax to Montreal. An online search will quickly reveal such opportunities, though not often far in advance.

Activities

- National parks offer a great array of choices for those who love breathtaking scenery and outdoor activities. If you like kayaking, paddle boarding or mountain biking, rent the gear outside of national parks for more budget-friendly options. For example, the University of Calgary rent summer and winter camping gear and equipment for outdoor activities.

- Doing some online research before your trip will save both time and money when you get there.

Food

- When going from a big city to the Rocky Mountains, stock up on supplies from a major supermarket first. Most of the larger supermarket chains have many options for prepared food and some will even heat it up for you in the deli section.

- Most city parks and campsites have barbecue grills that can be used by anyone. You only need to buy aluminium trays and whatever food you would like to grill.

Questions 8–14

Do the following statements agree with the information given in Reading Passage 1?

In boxes 8–14 on your answer sheet, write

TRUE	*if the statement agrees with the information*
FALSE	*if the statement contradicts the information*
NOT GIVEN	*if there is no information on this*

8 Train and bus fares cost the same amount.

9 Fees for hire cars usually cover the cost of insuring the vehicle.

10 Deals for relocating vehicles are only in major cities.

11 Deals to relocate vehicles tend to come up close to the time of departure.

12 National parks are the cheapest option for hiring outdoor equipment.

13 Warm food is available at some supermarkets.

14 Public parks often have facilities for cooking food.

You should spend about 20 minutes on **Questions 15–27**, which are based on Reading Passage 2.

Read the text below and answer **Questions 15–21**.

Dealing with customer complaints: a guide for Gray's Discount sales staff

An opportunity to improve

While we do our best to provide our customers with top-quality products and service, there will inevitably be occasional complaints. We need to look at these complaints as opportunities to make things right. The vast majority of customers who complain have reasonable grounds for doing so and we should be grateful that they do; the majority of unhappy customers will not make a complaint to us but will instead make it known to approximately ten people, as well as possibly complaining online.

A professional approach

Some complaints can be delivered forcefully and angrily. It is a challenge to remain calm in such situations, but this is what we, as staff, must do. It is worth bearing in mind that we shouldn't turn it into a personal matter; just address the issue at hand. Take a professional approach if a customer becomes agitated and keep your own emotions in check. This does not mean you should allow a customer to become abusive in any way – seek assistance from your manager if this occurs.

Finding out what's wrong

Listen carefully and attentively to what the customer has to say and let them finish. Sometimes people just want to be heard. Ensure you know the exact nature of the problem and show the customer you want to know what happened; the best way of doing this is to ask questions. Before you can present the customer with options for a solution, you need to check with them that you have a clear picture of why they are complaining.

Providing solutions

When the customer has given you all the details, be sure to acknowledge the issue (this does not necessarily mean accepting full blame). If the customer has not opened an item or the item is faulty, give them a replacement if that is what they request. There is no need to have this approved by a manager but note it in the diary in the office and put faulty items in the returns bay. However, if the customer requests a refund, you will need to have this processed by management.

In the case of ongoing or more serious complaints, it may be wise to follow up with a phone call or email to make sure the customer is satisfied with the outcome.

Complete the notes below.

Choose **ONE WORD ONLY** from the text for each answer.

Write your answers in boxes 15–21 on your answer sheet.

Dealing with customer complaints

Background

– Customers usually have good reasons to complain.

– Most dissatisfied customers don't complain to store but tell around **15** .... others and complain on the internet.

Manner

– Stay calm.

– Remember not to make it **16** ....

– Control your **17** .... during conflict.

Steps

– Listen to the customer.

– Allow the customer to **18** ....

– **19** .... can be used to show you're interested.

– **20** .... your understanding of the complaint.

– Acknowledge the problem.

– Offer a solution – **21** .... can be given without asking the manager.

– Must ask the manager for other transactions.

– Follow up if appropriate.

*Read Reading Passage 2 and answer **Questions 22–27**.*

Safety gear in the construction industry – the responsibility of employers and employees

Even in a highly-regulated area of work, accidents can still occur. Safety precautions must be in place to limit these accidents, and enforcing the wearing of safety gear can make the world of difference.

Employers must

- ensure that safety gear (see below) is worn by all workers on site.
- provide safety gear that is suitable for the nature of the work being done.
- provide safety gear of an appropriate size for each worker.
- ensure employees are trained and instructed in how to use / wear safety gear correctly.

Employees must

- wear safety gear in the course of their work on site.
- not misuse or intentionally cause damage to safety gear.
- inform the employer if safety gear is worn out or damaged.

Head	Hard hats are compulsory at all times on site to shield the head from falling objects and bumps. They also offer protection from rain, direct sun and electric shocks. Hard hats and helmets are available with built-in ventilation for those working underground or in tight spaces.
Eyes	This is a sensitive area, requiring the utmost protection, whether that be goggles or a transparent visor attached to a helmet.
	Protection should always be worn when working around smoke, extreme winds or in an area where hazardous chemicals are used or kept.
Body	Reflective safety vests are used to ensure high visibility on site. They may also be flame-retardant and breathable as the situation demands.
Hands	Almost all construction work requires the active use of hands; hence, proper precautions are required to avoid common injuries. Well-fitting safety gloves help protect hands from the most common hazard: lacerations. Other dangers include temperature extremes or anything that causes burns.
Feet	Closed-toe shoes with steel caps are a must to protect against falling objects, dangerous substances and heavy equipment. Rubber soles are also advised as many accidents happen due to slips.

Questions 22–27

Complete the sentences below.

*Choose **ONE WORD ONLY** from the text for each answer.*

Write your answers in boxes 22–27 on your answer sheet.

22 Employers in the construction industry have to make sure that workers have safety gear that is the right ....

23 Head gear may come with .... for enclosed places.

24 Employees working with dangerous .... need to protect their eyes.

25 .... and, therefore, safety is improved by wearing a reflective vest.

26 Burns to the hands occur less frequently than ....

27 .... can be avoided by wearing the proper footwear.

You should spend about 20 minutes on **Questions 28–40**, which are based on Reading Passage 3.

Read the text below and answer **Questions 28–40**.

The Comic Store

The Comic Store in Canterbury, UK, is a specialist bookshop established in 2008 by The Kent Consortium co-founder, Joe Lane. As well as establishing The Comic Store itself, Lane donated dozens of pieces of artwork from his private collection to decorate the walls and provide a permanent exhibition. The 8,000 m² building was designed by the well-known Hungarian architect, Zoltan Nagy.

It contains several display areas and has held many successful temporary exhibitions, some of which have since toured across Europe and internationally.

The Comic Store was formerly called the Cartoon Archive Project (CAP). Kasper Andersen, the curator at the time of the name change, explained that, besides art exhibits, the museum has a manga wing and has branched out into other areas of illustration and video, such as political cartoons, video games and contemporary art. Therefore, the new name was brought in to reflect the shop's move beyond single pieces of art to a wider range of comic-based media and artefacts.

The look and design of the store itself has been controversial with architects and the public debating whether it is beautiful or ugly. There has been much discussion about whether the modern building is in harmony with the surrounding historical buildings. Jade Lane, the sister of the founder who was involved in setting up the store, noted that it was important for the customer's experience to begin before they enter the building. The front of the building is decorated with large cartoon characters. The structure has many curves and shiny surfaces in various colours and materials, and its appearance has been compared to that of an eye watching the sky. Indeed, Nagy and his team took inspiration for the exterior of the building from the renowned artist Roy Lichtenstein's eye images. The mix of textures and colours used in the design is said to reflect the energy and fluidity of comic art.

The building project made technological advances in its sophisticated use of computer modelling which translated a three-dimensional shape into a geometric language that the project's engineers and builders could understand. The computer coordinates gave precise three-dimensional instructions – a critical point because the project had no straight, ruled surfaces. This resulted in a perfect fit when it was finally assembled which overcame some of the initial design challenges.

The hub of activity at The Comic Store is the presentation area called The Main Event. This space has a soaring ceiling, state-of-the art acoustics and lighting, along with an IMAX screen that is one of the largest in the UK. As well as being a venue for private events, workshops and presentations, it is sometimes open late to the public for experiences such as *The Comic Sleepover*, where visitors can bring their own cushions and enjoy a series of classic cartoons.

The Comic Store offers a wide variety of exhibitions, comics, books and mechandise for those interested in cartoons. Its largest exhibition to date has been *Superheroes Save the Day* on the second floor of the store.

This features models of superheroes, such as Spiderman, Dr Who and Wonderwoman, as well as the chance to see authentic comics dating back to the 1930's. Set next to this on the second floor is the DC Thomson exhibition, which pays homage to the famous Dundee design company which created those famous comics *The Beano* and *The Dandy*. Visitors can explore photos, cartoons and, if eager to see more, can go to dedicated kiosks to watch videos. Just across from this, The Levels offers an insight into gaming history, featuring the stories of video game developers, designers, coders, composers and critics. Also, on this floor, the *Make-believe* exhibition showcases items from lands of fantasy, such as a replica of Gandalf the Wizard's staff (stick) from *Lord of the Rings,* one of the dragon models from *Harry Potter* and maps from *Star Trek*.

Besides the exhibitions themselves, there are many dedicated spaces at the Comic Store that are set aside and available to be booked for educational workshops or entertainment purposes. For example, The Hive is a flexible space with a moveable air wall that means it can be subdivided into several rooms.

Seminars are held there, and it can be booked privately, as can the Outdoor Terrace which can be setup for events, offering a pleasant outlook over some of the city's points of interest such as the Cathedral or City Walls.

The Comic Store employs more than 50 people, most – if not all – of whom have experience and training in design, visual art and/or writing. In addition, there are many volunteers who share their knowledge and enthusiasm with visitors. Several internships are also offered every year to those who are hoping for a career in the arts or arts-based retail, but these positions are quite highly sought after so there is a long waiting list. More positions are, however, expected to be created in future as the The Comic Store attracts 50,000 visitors a year.

Questions 28–32

*Look at the following statements, **Questions 28–32**, and the areas of The Comic Store below.*

*Match each statement with the correct part of The Comic Store, **A, B, C** or **D**.*

*Write the correct letter, **A, B, C** or **D**, in boxes 28–32 on your answer sheet.*

***NB** you may use any letter more than once.*

28   It has views of Canterbury's landmarks.

29   It can be booked for large parties.

30   The area can be adjusted to create smaller spaces.

31   It hosts film events outside the usual opening hours.

32   Its design was influenced by the shape of a body part.

Areas of The Comic Store
A Exterior
B The Main Event
C Outdoor Terrace
D The Hive

Choose the correct letter, **A, B, C** *or* **D**.

Write the correct letter in boxes 33–36 on your answer sheet.

33 What does the writer say in the first paragraph about the exhibitions at *The Comic Store*?

    A Some of them have been shown in other cities.

    B They often reflect the architecture of the building.

    C They were commissioned by the store's founder.

    D Visitors to *The Comic Store* are allowed to touch most things on display.

34 The name of the shop was changed to *The Comic Store*

    A as the public did not like the former name.

    B because it sounded good and was and easier to remember.

    C in order to signal a change in the management of the shop.

    D to show the shop had a wider focus than its earlier name suggested.

35 What does the writer say in the third paragraph about the construction of *The Comic Store*?

    A The architect chose a construction team he had worked with before.

    B The people who built it were helped by the use of computer design.

    C A famous optician was consulted about the way it looked.

    D Engineers found it difficult to make the design a reality.

36 What does the writer say about the staff at *The Comic Store*?

    A A high proportion of them are volunteers.

    B Many of them have creative backgrounds.

    C Employees tend to stay in their jobs for a long time.

    D Working as an intern can lead to full-time employment at the stop.

Questions 37–40

Label the map.

Choose **ONE WORD ONLY** *from the text for each answer.*

Write your answers in boxes 37–40 on your answer sheet.

The Comic Store

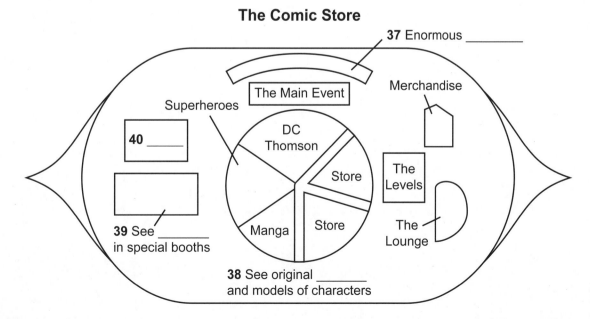

37 Enormous _____

The Main Event

Superheroes

Merchandise

DC Thomson

40 _____

Store

The Levels

39 See _____ in special booths

Manga

Store

The Lounge

38 See original _____ and models of characters

Writing Task 1

You should spend about 20 minutes on this task.

You recently had something delivered to your home. You now realise the person who delivered it damaged something in your home while they were delivering the item.

Write a letter to the manager of the delivery company. In your letter:
- *give details of the delivery*
- *describe what was damaged*
- *say what you would like the manager to do*

Write at least 150 words.

You do **NOT** need to write any addresses.

Begin your letter as follows:

Dear ....,

Writing Task 2

You should spend about 40 minutes on this task.

Write about the following topic:

More and more people are moving from rural areas to live in cities.

What problems can this cause?

How can these problems be solved?

Give reasons for your answer and include any relevant examples from your own knowledge or experience.

Write at least 250 words.

Speaking Part 1

The examiner will start by introducing him/herself and checking your identity. He or she will then ask you some questions about yourself and then go on to ask you some questions about one or two other topics, for example:

Let's talk about mobile/cell phones.

- *When did you get your first mobile/cell phone?*
- *How often do you change your mobile/cell phone?*
- *What do you use it for most often?*
- *Do you think you could live without a mobile/cell phone?*

or

Let's talk about concentrating.

- *When do you need to concentrate most?*
- *Do you ever find it difficult to concentrate?*
- *What do you do to help you concentrate?*
- *Did you find it easier or harder to concentrate when you were younger?*

Speaking Part 2

The examiner will give you a topic like the one below and some paper and a pencil.

The examiner will say:

I'm going to give you a topic and I'd like you to talk about it for one to two minutes. Before you talk, you'll have one minute to think about what you're going to say. You can make some notes if you wish.   [1 minute]

All right? Remember you have one to two minutes for this, so don't worry if I stop you. I'll tell you when the time is up. Can you start speaking now, please?

Describe a person you know who has an interesting job.

You should say:
   who the person is
   what job the person does
   what skills he or she needs to do this job

and explain why you think this person's job is interesting.

The examiner may ask one or two rounding-off questions when you have finished your talk, for example:
- *Have you told other people about this person?*
- *Do you think you would be good at this person's job?*

Speaking Part 3

The examiner will ask some general questions which are connected to the topic in Part 2. You will usually have to answer up to six questions.

The examiner will say, for example:

We've been talking about a person you know who has an interesting job. I'd like to discuss with you one or two more general questions relating to this. First, let's consider choosing a job.

- *Who can best advise young people about jobs, parents or teachers? Why?*
- *What is the most important thing to consider when choosing a job?*

Let's talk about different ways of working now.

- *Is it better to work for a small company or a large international company? Why?*
- *What are the advantages and disadvantages of working from home?*

Finally, let's talk about having a successful career.

- *Many people say that learning from mistakes is the key to a successful career. Do you agree with this view?*
- *How easy is it for people who want a successful career to balance their work and personal life?*

Questions 1–10

Complete the table below.

Write **ONE WORD ONLY AND / OR A NUMBER** *for each answer.*

Kingstown Tours

Name of tour	Price	Main activities	Other information
Cave Explorers	*Example* *$93*	• go in a small **1** ....~~train~~...... to the other side of the lake • explore the caves	• minimum age of **2** ...~~5~~..... years
Silver Fjord	$220	• travel by **3** ...~~Coach~~... to the fjord *Coach* • at Easten go for a **4** ...~~walk~~........ • cruise on the fjord • see mountains and a large **5** ...~~waterfall~~...	• eat a barbecue lunch • see marine life such as seals and **6** ...~~whales~~...... *dolphins*
High Country	$105	• visit a historic home • lunch is in the **7** ...~~garden~~........ • in the afternoon visit a **8** ...~~farm~~......	• this tour has excellent reviews
Zipline	$75	• travel on a zipline above an old **9** ...~~wire~~...... *safe.*	• reach speeds of **10** ...~~68~~......... *(43)* miles per hour

forest

waterfall

Questions 11–15

31

*Choose the correct letter, **A**, **B** or **C**.*

Willford Living Museum

11 In the early 1800s most land in Willford was
   A occupied by houses.
   B used for farming.
   C covered in trees.

12 What happened in 1830 in Willford?
   A Ships started to be built nearby.
   B The first trains arrived in the town.
   C Valuable substances were found underground.

13 By the 1870s Willford was most famous for making
   A various metal objects.
   B all types of clothing. ?
   C plates and cups.

14 What does the guide say about visitors to the museum these days?
   A 900 visitors enter on a typical day.
   B 7,600 visitors arrive every week.
   C 300,000 visitors come each year.

15 The museum is also sometimes used
   A as a location for filming.
   B for business conferences.
   C by people getting married.

Questions 16–20

Label the map below.

*Write the correct letter, **A–H**, next to **Questions 16–20**.*

Willford Living Museum

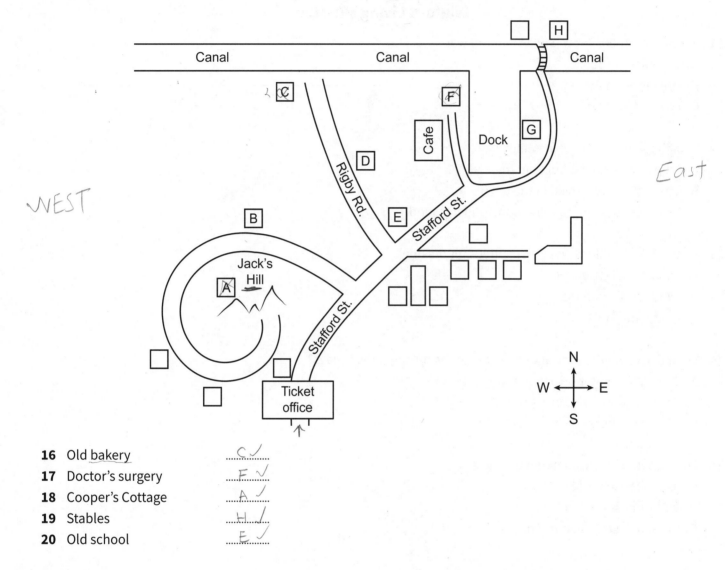

16 Old bakery ....C ✓.........
17 Doctor's surgery ....F ✓.........
18 Cooper's Cottage ....A ✓.........
19 Stables ....H ✓.........
20 Old school ....E ✓.........

Questions 21–22

*Choose **TWO** letters, **A–E**.*

*According to the students, what are the **TWO** most important benefits of market research?*

A Selecting the best advertising
B Reducing the levels of risks
C Building confidence among employees
D Saving money in the long run
E Identifying new opportunities

Questions 23–24

*Choose **TWO** letters, **A–E**.*

*Which do the students agree are **TWO** valid criticisms of market research?*

A It does not reveal any new information.
B Its benefits are hard to measure.
C It takes too much time to carry out.
D It makes use of too much specialist language.
E Its findings are sometimes wrong.

Questions 25–26

*Choose **TWO** letters, **A–E**.*

*The students are surprised by the success of which **TWO** sources of information.*

A face-to-face communication
B official government statistics
C the media and social media
D online surveys of public opinion
E filming customers as they shop

Questions 27–30

Complete the flow-chart below.

*Choose **FOUR** answers from the box and write the correct letter, **A–F**, next to **Questions 27–30**.*

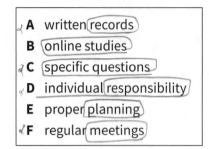

A written records
B online studies
C specific questions
D individual responsibility
E proper planning
F regular meetings

Market Research Using a Business's Own Resources

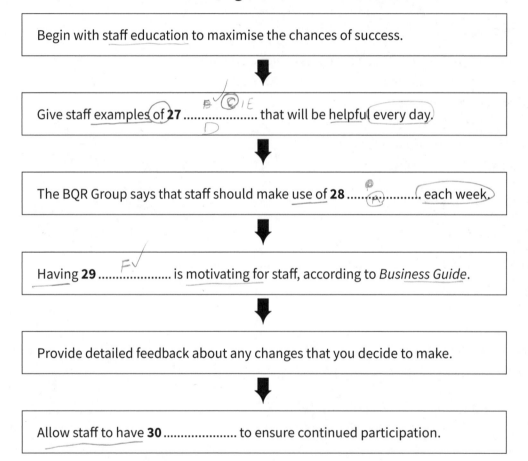

Begin with staff education to maximise the chances of success.

⬇

Give staff examples of **27** .... that will be helpful every day.

⬇

The BQR Group says that staff should make use of **28** .... each week.

⬇

Having **29** .... is motivating for staff, according to *Business Guide*.

⬇

Provide detailed feedback about any changes that you decide to make.

⬇

Allow staff to have **30** .... to ensure continued participation.

Questions 31–37

33

Complete the notes below.

*Write **ONE WORD ONLY** for each answer.*

Drinking Water

Introduction

- Drinking water is essential for human life.
- The '8 glasses a day' rule is a myth, except for the **31** ....   *elderly* ✓

Some effects of water on the body

- Drinking before **32** .... may assist weight loss.   *wake up*
- Dr Amaldi's study shows that water speeds up **33** ....   *stomach* / *digestion*
- A US research study showed that dehydrated bodies cannot control **34** .... so well.   *temperature* ✓
- There is no evidence that drinking water results in better **35** ....   *skin*

The brain

- Women who drank lots of water had fewer **36** ....   *headaches* ✓
- Men suffered more **37** .... with insufficient water.   *anxiety* ✓

Questions 38–40

Complete the summary below.

*Write **ONE WORD ONLY** for each answer.*

---

   swallowing

Too much water?

Drinking too much water is not a common problem. Australian research has shown that people have difficulty **38** .... when they have drunk enough. But occasionally people have become sick from too much water, particularly groups of **39** .... *athletes* This may be because they have high levels of **40** .... in their *advice* blood. The best advice is to drink when you are thirsty.   *hyp* / *salt*

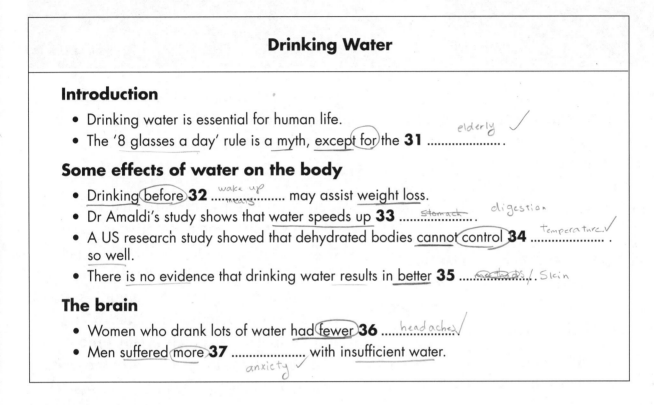

---

*You should spend about 20 minutes on **Questions 1–14**, which are based on the two texts below.*

*Read the text below and answer **Questions 1–7**.*

What's on?
Sydney's Night Noodle Markets

The Night Noodle Markets are returning to Hyde Park, serving up the best street food Sydney has to offer. You'll see old favourites as well as new contenders, and while the focus is still firmly on Asian cuisine, European and South American delicacies also feature.

The usual suspects are back this year, with stalls such as **Hoy Pinoy** and **Mr Bao** promising to deliver the delicious fare the city has come to look forward to. **Black Star Pastry** is also back, by popular demand.

As usual, there will be no shortage of noodle options. Don't miss **Taiwanese Noodle House** and its brisket noodle soup.

But the market does a lot more than noodles; the much-loved **Indu** restaurant has a stall serving the South Indian dosa, a crisp pancake. Join the queue for a dosa filled with goat meat and pomegranate or, if you don't eat meat, try the eggplant with bitter melon.

More than just food

The market space called **Hyde Park Palms** offers plenty of entertainment, from popular DJs to family-friendly live music. Illuminated dragons roam throughout the market until 10p.m. Check the Noodle Market website for details of the line-up.

Tips:

- Come early – the later you arrive, the longer the lines and the more chance of a stall running out of your first choice of dish. Stalls are well-stocked this year, but demand is high for the favourites, so don't be disappointed. The lines for the most popular stalls such as **Hoy Pinoy** and **Indu** can be long, but worth the wait.

- Beanbags and chairs around tables are the only seating options provided and they can be hard to come by at this busy event – consider bringing your own rug.

- If the weather looks suspect, check our website before heading out. As a rule, the market will go ahead unless it is pouring with rain.

- It's a cash-free event, so bring your plastic. Put it on your card and don't worry about counting out change.

Questions 1–7

Do the following statements agree with the information given in Reading Passage 1?

In boxes 1–7 on your answer sheet, write

TRUE	*if the statement agrees with the information*
FALSE	*if the statement contradicts the information*
NOT GIVEN	*if there is no information on this*

1 The market specialises in food cooked in an Asian style. T
2 This is the first time Black Star Pastry is taking part in the festival. F
3 The vegetarian option from Indu is more popular than the meat option. N G
4 The entertainment starts early in the evening. N.G
5 Hoy Pinoy is one of the busiest stalls at the market. T
6 The festival supplies rugs for people to sit on. F
7 Stalls at the night market can process payments made by card. T

Read the text below and answer **Questions 8–14**.

Tips for managing your time

A To see how you currently manage your time, it's useful to keep a log of everything you do. Start by writing down what you do every 30-minutes for a week – you may be surprised at what you see. Ask yourself when you are the most productive, what you devote most of your time to and how long your routine activities take.

B Make a list of everything you need to do. Include everything, large and small, and add to it as you go. At this stage, it isn't necessary to assign priorities and times; just capture your ideas before you forget them.

C A long list of things to do is just the first step. Once you've made your list, it's time to prioritise tasks. Put them in order of urgency and how much value it will bring you to have them done. Then you will be better able to allocate the right amount of time to each task.

D Remember that scheduling is not only writing down what you have to do, it is also making time for the things you want to do. You should make room for family and friends or pursuing creative interests and sport, just as you would for chores and work / study responsibilities.

E Look back at your log and reflect on the times you are most productive – and then schedule your tasks according to their priority and your energy levels.

F While using a conventional list on paper might be a good way to get started, you might find software is more helpful. You can get apps to send you reminders, merge your calendar with those of colleagues, as well as helping you delete and prioritise tasks.

G Most people find that disorganisation results in poor time management. Clear your home and workspace of clutter that is draining your energy and diverting your concentration. Many people find it useful to have three piles: *Keep*, *Give away* and *Throw in the rubbish*. When a task has been dealt with, file it (either physically or digitally) somewhere you can easily find it again.

Questions 8–14

*The reading text above has seven sections, **A–G**.*

Which section mentions the following?

*Write the correct letter, **A–G**, in boxes 8–14 on your answer sheet.*

NB *You may use any letter more than once.*

8   why it might be better to use technology

9   how to keep a record of the ways you spend your time

10   why you should mark things in order of importance on your list

11   how to get rid of things that distract you

12   what types of activities you need to plan

13   how to decide when to do a task

14   what to do with work you have completed

*You should spend about 20 minutes on **Questions 15–27**, which are based on Reading Passage 2.*

*Read the text and answer **Questions 15–21**.*

Starting a new business: points to consider

Starting a business can mean a huge change in lifestyle and also a large financial commitment. However, it is possible to be ready for this if you are well prepared from the start. We've put together some tips to help you:

Evaluate your idea

You may believe you have a great idea, but you need to ask yourself if the present market demands it; gather and analyse information to establish the feasibility of your business.

Make a plan

Doing this will mean that you clarify goals for the business and what you will do to achieve them. Always be generous in your costing to allow for unforeseen circumstances; it's safest to consider the worst-case scenario.

Business models

You need to select the business structure that is most suitable for your purposes. Take professional advice if you are unsure. Here are some examples:

- sole trader – an individual trading on their own
- partnership – a number of people or entities running a business together
- company – a legal entity that is separate from its owners

Analyse yourself

Operating a business is not just about being self-employed. There are many questions to ask yourself in order to be sure that running a business is the best option for you, and you need to be honest with yourself from the beginning.

- Why do you want to have your own business?
- Do you have the right temperament to deal with challenges and possible setbacks?
- Do you have management skills and expertise in the industry?
- What are your personal strengths, and, on the flipside, what weaknesses may you need to overcome?

What if …?

You need to consider potential problems before they occur.

- Do you need to have your product patented? You don't want anyone stealing your invention. If it's a new product or process, speak to a patent attorney to make sure your idea is protected.
- Who will run the business when you can't? Many small business owners want to do everything themselves, but eventually everyone needs to take holidays and family demands may take them away from the business. Do you have good staff you can trust to keep the business going in your absence?
- Will your business be able to withstand emergencies? Check you have insurance that covers you and your business for anything that could possibly go wrong, from theft, to natural disaster, to ill health.

Questions 15–21

Complete the sentences below.

Write **ONE WORD ONLY** from the text for each answer.

Write the answers in boxes 15–21 on your answer sheet.

15 Before investing in a new business, do research about its ......*demands*....... in the current market.

16 Making a business plan will help you be clear about your ....*goals*..........

17 Choose the .....*structure*.... which best matches how you want to run your business.

18 In terms of your personality, ask yourself if your .... allows you to manage difficult situations.

19 Be aware of any .....*weaknesses*.... you have, as well as the skills and qualities you possess.

20 You may need to look into ways of ensuring the ....*running*....... of your business idea.

21 You should make sure your plan includes .....*insurance*.... to safeguard against problems in future.

*Read the text below and answer **Questions 22–27**.*

Hay and Walford Ltd: Social Media Policy for employees

Here at Hay and Walford Ltd, we acknowledge the role social media plays in shaping our public image and the image our clients and associates have of us.

Whether on our official company accounts or workers' individual social media accounts, we encourage all employees to bear in mind that they represent the firm and comments remain on the internet long after they were first made.

Company social media accounts

You do not know the influence a throwaway remark may have. For this reason, please refrain from commenting on any litigation that the company is involved in.

Similarly, anything that is labelled 'for internal use only' is not to be shared in full or in part on social media.

Messages from the CEO are automatically confidential and should not be mentioned in social media posts.

The company's finances are especially sensitive information and must not be shared, commented on or speculated on at all.

If you make an error of fact or wish to review your professional opinion, please take immediate steps to make corrections or delete the post.

Bear in mind that we are bound by regulations relating to copyright. As such, do not share the work of other people or companies without correctly acknowledging them as creators.

To be on the safe side, if you are in any doubt as to whether to put something on our social media accounts, please do not post in the first instance and seek advice from one of the team in Communications about whether the information is sensitive or unsuitable from the company's point of view.

Individual accounts

Even via private accounts, employees can be associated with the company.

If you wish to mention the company but are not an official spokesperson for Hay and Walford Ltd, make it clear what your position in the company is.

Whether discussing company business or not, be aware that comments made by employees that contradict our values of equality and decency can reflect badly on the company. We ask that you always treat other users of social media with respect, whatever the situation.

To the extent that your image on social media is public, it needs to be in line with the professional image that you, and Hay and Walford Ltd, wish to present.

Complete the notes below.

*Choose **ONE WORD ONLY** from the text for each answer.*

Write your answers in boxes 22–27 on your answer sheet.

Hay and Walford Ltd: Social Media Policy for employees

Hay and Walford's official social media accounts

- Never post about:
  - **22** ....~~litigation~~.... that is currently taking place.
  - matters marked 'for internal use only'.
  - anything that relates to the company's **23** ....~~finances~~....
- Correct / delete any misinformation immediately.
- Observe the **24** ....~~copyright~~.... of other brands and individuals.
- Consult **25** ....~~team~~.... if unsure about appropriacy of post.

Employees' private accounts

- If discussing the company:
  - must state your role unless you are a company **26** ....~~spokesperson~~....
- If not discussing company:
  - still need to show **27** ....~~respect~~....
- Ensure private accounts are consistent with professional image.

You should spend about 20 minutes on **Questions 28–40**, which are based on Reading Passsage 3.

Read the text on page 176 and answer **Questions 28–40**.

Questions 28–32

The text above has five sections, **A–E**.

Choose the correct heading for each paragraph from the list of headings below.

Write the correct number, **i–vi**, in boxes 28–32 on your answer sheet.

NB you may use any letter more than once.

28   Section A   ii

29   Section B   i

30   Section C   4

31   Section D   6

32   Section E   iii

List of Headings

i   Using kites for scientific research

ii   Types of kite

iii Factors that determine whether a kite will fly

iv   The beginning of manned flight

v   The popularity of kites throughout the years

vi   Basic features shared by all kites

Reasons :
initial, start
famous
All kites -same

The history of kites

A

The fighter kite is an ancient design that became popular in Asia. While there were some variations, fighter kites tended to be small, flat and diamond-shaped and were flown throughout Asia, including in Japan and India. The main part of this kite was made of paper, while its spine consisted of a piece of tapered bamboo. There was also a rounded, balanced bow. These kites did not have tails, which were thought to affect their manoeuvrability. Most of the line was made of cotton but part of this was covered with an abrasive, which could cut an opponent's line in a competition.

European kites developed later, possibly crafted out of flags. Nowadays there are eight main kinds of kite worldwide: the flat, bowed, box, sled, delta and compound, all of which have frames, and now the parafoil which is somewhat like a parachute, and the rotor which has a spinning vane between two cylinders. Perhaps most significantly, the materials used to build kites remained basically unchanged for hundreds of years, but today the materials that comprise the various components of kites are often synthetic.

B *science*

In Europe, kites were curiosities at first rather than being part of the culture, but they were soon used as vehicles for discovery and innovation. In 1893, William A Eddy introduced a tailless kite that was in the shape of an elongated diamond. He was interested in the potential kites had for the purposes of meteorology and aerial photography. Besides being responsible for a renewed interest in kite-flying throughout Europe, Eddy's kite was also utilised by the United States Weather Bureau.

In 1752, the American inventor and statesman Benjamin Franklin went out in a thunderstorm with his son to fly a flat kite with a pointed wire. They attached a metal key to the kite's line and watched as it became electrified, both miraculously avoiding electrocution. This proved that lightning was a natural occurrence called electricity, and this experiment led to Franklin inventing the lightning rod, a metallic rod that protects a structure from lightning damage by guiding currents from lightning flashes into the ground.

C *manned*

Kites also contributed greatly to the development of the airplane. The first recorded aircraft with a person inside was British aviator Sir George Cayley's glider in 1853. He used modified kites to test whether his glider idea would work. This was a big step in aviation, as it dispelled the former assumption that an aircraft would need wings that flapped like a bird's.

Around 1900 Orville and Wilbur Wright started using kites to test their ideas for planes. These brothers ran a bicycle shop in Ohio in the United States and were obsessed with aviation. It was the Wright brothers who concentrated on how to control the aircraft, something that had, until then, baffled many other inventors. The Wright brothers made a box kite that was wired in a way that meant the kite could be made to turn. Not long after that, they successfully flew the first manned airplane. Without experiments with kites, modern aircraft would have taken much longer to be developed.

D *features*

Whatever the design of a kite, in order to fly, it needs to have certain characteristics. Firstly, it needs to be able to lift in the wind and this requires an aerodynamic structure. It also needs to have something that stops it from flying away; this is called a tether. One end of the tether is connected to the kite and the other is usually on a hand-held spool for a person to manage the length of the line. Another necessary component is the bridle, which is two or more lines that are attached to each other at a point and this can be adjusted according to the strength and direction of the wind.

E

There are three forces that control kite flight; these are lift, gravity and drag. If the wind is stronger than the resistance of the air (drag) and the pull of gravity, the kite should be able to fly. One way in which a kite differs from a plane is that when the kite is fixed (using the tether) so that the wind gives it lift, it maintains what is called 'perpetual stall'. This is essential for a kite to fly but would not be a suitable design for an aeroplane. If a kite is flat, it should have a tail to provide drag so that the nose of the kite is pointing upwards.

Although many people try it, running with a kite is not an effective way to send it into the sky. It is better to start off with two people, one holding the kite and the other with the line unravelled about 30 metres, holding the reel or spool. The bridle of the kite should be facing the person who is not holding it and the breeze should come from behind the kite. If all this has been done, the kite should be launched successfully when the person holding it lets go of it.

Questions 33–36

Label the diagram below.

*Choose **ONE WORD ONLY** from the text for each answer.*

Write your answers in boxes 33–36 on your answer sheet.

Fighter Kite

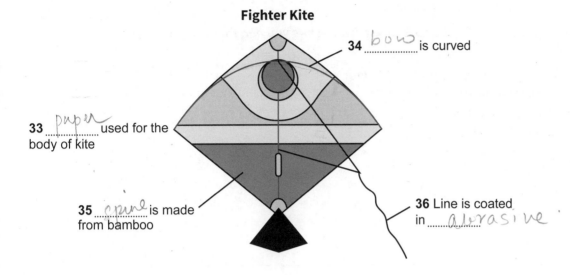

33 *paper* used for the body of kite

34 *bow* is curved

35 *spine* is made from bamboo

36 Line is coated in *abrasive*

Questions 37–40

*Choose the correct letter, **A, B, C** or **D**.*

Write the correct letter in boxes 37–40 on your answer sheet.

37 What is the main difference between kites in the past and modern kites?

   A Their parts are made from different substances.

   B Modern kites tend to be larger.

   C Kites in the past were less sturdy.

   D They are used for different purposes.

38 Benjamin Franklin's experience flying a kite in a storm

   A led to a useful innovation.

   B proved it was not a dangerous thing to do.

   C showed that his son's theory was correct.

   D was a successful use of a new kind of kite.

39 The Wright Brothers differed from other early aviation engineers in that they

   A used kites as models for real planes.

   B worked on how to determine the direction of a kite.

   C applied what they had learned in their bicycle business to flying.

   D made an important discovery by accident.

40 The best way to send a kite into the air is to

   A hold the kite and run along with it.

   B ensure that the wind blows underneath the kite.

   C release the kite at a distance from a person holding the string.

   D let the kite fly from a person's hand as it is given more string.

Exam Practice Test 6 | Writing Tasks 1–2

Writing Task 1

You should spend about 20 minutes on this task.

You recently borrowed an item of clothing from a friend. While you had this item, it was damaged.

Write a letter to your friend. In your letter you should:
- *apologise for damaging the item of clothing*
- *explain how it became damaged*
- *say what you will do to fix the problem*

Write at least 150 words.

You do **NOT** need to write any addresses.

Begin your letter as follows:

Dear ....,

Writing Task 2

You should spend about 40 minutes on this task.

Write about the following topic:

The best way to measure someone's success is to look at how much money that person has.

Do you agree or disagree with this statement?

Give reasons for your answer and include any relevant examples from your own knowledge or experience.

Write at least 250 words.

Speaking Part 1

The examiner will start by introducing him/herself and checking your identity. He or she will then ask you some questions about yourself and then go on to ask you some questions about one or two other topics, for example:

Let's talk about cars.

- *Do you like travelling by car?*
- *Is the colour of a car important to you?*
- *Do you prefer to drive or to be a passenger in a car?*
- *What kind of car would you like to have in the future?*

or

Let's talk about primary / elementary school.

- *What was the best thing about your primary / elementary school?*
- *Which subject did you <u>not</u> like at your primary / elementary school?*
- *Are you still in touch with some of your friends from primary / elementary school?*
- *In the future, would you like to send a child of yours to the same primary / elementary school?*

Speaking Part 2

The examiner will give you a topic like the one below and some paper and a pencil.

The examiner will say:

I'm going to give you a topic and I'd like you to talk about it for one to two minutes. Before you talk, you'll have one minute to think about what you're going to say. You can make some notes if you wish.   [1 minute]

All right? Remember you have one to two minutes for this, so don't worry if I stop you. I'll tell you when the time is up. Can you start speaking now, please?

Describe a song that you will always remember.

You should say:
> **what the song is**
> **when and where you first heard this song**
> **what you liked about this song**

and explain why you will always remember this song.

The examiner may ask one or two rounding-off questions when you have finished your talk, for example:

- *Do your friends like this song too?*
- *Do you listen to a lot of songs?*

Speaking Part 3

The examiner will ask some general questions which are connected to the topic in Part 2. You will usually have to answer up to six questions.

The examiner will say, for example:

We've been talking about a song that you will always remember. I'd like to discuss with you one or two more general questions relating to this. First, let's consider listening to music.

- *What types of music do young people in your country enjoy listening to?*
- *What is different about listening to music at home and going to a live concert?*

Let's talk about music in everyday life.

- *Why do so many people listen to music when they are travelling to work/college?*

Finally, let's talk about the future of music.

- *Should governments subsidise less popular forms of music such as opera? Why do you think that?*

Sample Answer Sheet for Listening

IELTS Listening Answer Sheet

Candidate Name	

Candidate No. ☐☐☐☐☐☐☐ **Centre No.** ☐☐☐☐☐

Test Date Day ☐☐ Month ☐☐ Year ☐☐☐☐

Listening Listening Listening Listening Listening Listening Listening

Marker use only

1		✓ 1 ✗
2		✓ 2 ✗
3		✓ 3 ✗
4		✓ 4 ✗
5		✓ 5 ✗
6		✓ 6 ✗
7		✓ 7 ✗
8		✓ 8 ✗
9		✓ 9 ✗
10		✓ 10 ✗
11		✓ 11 ✗
12		✓ 12 ✗
13		✓ 13 ✗
14		✓ 14 ✗
15		✓ 15 ✗
16		✓ 16 ✗
17		✓ 17 ✗
18		✓ 18 ✗
19		✓ 19 ✗
20		✓ 20 ✗

Marker use only

21		✓ 21 ✗
22		✓ 22 ✗
23		✓ 23 ✗
24		✓ 24 ✗
25		✓ 25 ✗
26		✓ 26 ✗
27		✓ 27 ✗
28		✓ 28 ✗
29		✓ 29 ✗
30		✓ 30 ✗
31		✓ 31 ✗
32		✓ 32 ✗
33		✓ 33 ✗
34		✓ 34 ✗
35		✓ 35 ✗
36		✓ 36 ✗
37		✓ 37 ✗
38		✓ 38 ✗
39		✓ 39 ✗
40		✓ 40 ✗

Marker 2 Signature: _____ Marker 1 Signature: _____ Listening Total: ☐☐

20656

Sample Answer Sheet for Reading

BRITISH COUNCIL **idp** **Cambridge Assessment English**

IELTS Reading Answer Sheet

Candidate Name

Candidate No.

Centre No.

Test Module ☐ Academic ☐ General Training

Test Date Day Month Year

Reading Reading Reading Reading Reading Reading Reading

	Marker use only			Marker use only
1	1 ✓ ✗	**21**	21 ✓ ✗
2	2 ✓ ✗	22	22 ✓ ✗
3	3 ✓ ✗	**23**	23 ✓ ✗
4	4 ✓ ✗	24	24 ✓ ✗
5	5 ✓ ✗	**25**	25 ✓ ✗
6	6 ✓ ✗	26	26 ✓ ✗
7	7 ✓ ✗	**27**	27 ✓ ✗
8	8 ✓ ✗	28	28 ✓ ✗
9	9 ✓ ✗	**29**	29 ✓ ✗
10	10 ✓ ✗	30	30 ✓ ✗
11	11 ✓ ✗	**31**	31 ✓ ✗
12	12 ✓ ✗	32	32 ✓ ✗
13	13 ✓ ✗	**33**	33 ✓ ✗
14	14 ✓ ✗	34	34 ✓ ✗
15	15 ✓ ✗	**35**	35 ✓ ✗
16	16 ✓ ✗	36	36 ✓ ✗
17	17 ✓ ✗	**37**	37 ✓ ✗
18	18 ✓ ✗	38	38 ✓ ✗
19	19 ✓ ✗	**39**	39 ✓ ✗
20	20 ✓ ✗	40	40 ✓ ✗

Marker 2 Signature:

Marker 1 Signature:

Reading Total:

61788

Sample Answer Sheet for Writing

BRITISH COUNCIL   **idp**   **Cambridge Assessment English**

IELTS Writing Answer Sheet - TASK 1

Candidate Name

Candidate No.   **Centre No.**

Test Module ☐ Academic ☐ General Training   **Test Date** Day ☐☐ Month ☐☐ Year ☐☐☐☐

If you need more space to write your answer, use an additional sheet and write in the space provided to indicate how many sheets you are using: Sheet ☐ of ☐

Writing   Task 1   Writing   Task 1   Writing   Task 1   Writing   Task 1

Do not write below this line

Do not write in this area. Please continue your answer on the other side of this sheet.

23505